GAZZA

in

ITALY

The cheers, the tears, the jeers, the beers.
The incredible story of Paul Gascoigne's
three years at Lazio.

DANIEL STOREY

HarperCollins*Publishers*

HarperCollins*Publishers*
1 London Bridge Street
London SE1 9GF

www.harpercollins.co.uk

First published by HarperCollins*Publishers* 2018

1 3 5 7 9 10 8 6 4 2

Daniel Storey asserts the moral right to be
identified as the author of this work

A catalogue record of this book is
available from the British Library

ISBN 978-0-00-830086-9

Printed and bound in Great Britain by
CPI Group (UK) Ltd, Croydon, CR0 4YY

MIX
Paper from
responsible sources
FSC™ C007454

This book is produced from independently certified FSC™ paper
to ensure responsible forest management.

For more information visit: www.harpercollins.co.uk/green

To Livvy,
whose patience with
football is stronger than
my obsession

CONTENTS

PREFAZIONE

by James Richardson

I first met Paul Gascoigne on the grassy slopes of the garden at the Hotel Cavalieri in Rome.

It's a magnificent spot – the hotel overlooking the Eternal City across a series of leafy lawns – and on that sweltering afternoon in August 1992 I was feeling the heat more than most as I prepared to meet the footballing phenomenon I'd been hired to babysit and produce for Channel 4's *Gazzetta Football Italia* programme.

The task was daunting. Unlike me, Paul was famous, successful and very good at kicking a football, one of the chief life skills any right-thinking boy should aspire to. Worse still, he was almost exactly my age. Clearly, he would soon be making me cry and dispensing Chinese burns on a regular basis.

Instead, Paul surprised me by shaking my hand warmly, and giving me a look that I was often to see: wary, but also ever-eager for an audience. And so we began a polite friendship, one that lasted for precisely the amount of time that he was in Italy.

We were very different, but while he was there we had two things in common: our new life in the sweaty bustle of Rome, and our weekly commitment to filming his TV links and diary entry for Channel 4's Saturday-morning Italian round-up.

The filming went tits-up just a few weeks in, as Paul missed our appointment by a day or two. Timing was always an issue with him – perhaps his own way of finding some freedom within the intense bubble in which he lived. It mattered little, though. Whenever he was with you, you'd forgive him anything.

Paul was always generous and down to earth. He constantly seemed to want everyone around him to be happy – as long as it didn't require his punctuality. We'd film his segments, and then, because the life of a footballer isn't actually that exciting a topic, we'd try and improvise some theatrics to include in the show. This always brought out the best in Paul. Whether putting his entire head inside an Easter egg or waking up alongside me holding a kitchen whisk as a sex toy, he was game for anything for the camera – and most things off it.

The years he spent in Italy were not without their ups and downs, and featured yet another serious leg injury – this one in training, courtesy of a fresh-faced Lazio teenager called Alessandro Nesta. His time there was ended finally by the arrival of possibly the single worst manager Paul could ever encounter, Zdeněk Zeman, whose rigorous tactics and utter commitment to player fitness were the antithesis of Gazza's own plastic-tits-out charm. Paul departed Rome for Glasgow soon after, leaving behind a feeling that although this city had loved him more than any other, it never really saw the best of him.

Perhaps. For that brief spell though, Paul gave Lazio's fans so much to delight them. His goal in the Rome derby cemented his place in Laziali hearts and his mazy slalom against Pescara a place in club legend. Meanwhile, his irreverent style meant that – uniquely – this was a player loved by fans on both sides of the Tiber. '*Ubriacone, con l'orecchino, vieni qua e facci un pompino*', Roma's fans would sing at the Stadio Olimpico, with words ill-suited to translation here, but when out with Paul in Rome they would be the first to run to salute him: '*Grande Gazza! Sei un mito!*'

It's a pleasure to look back now on the joy that period brought, when Gazza was just a supremely talented young man doing what he did best.

NOTTI MAGICHE

Italia 90 and the making of Gazzamania

The thirty-one days between 8 June and 8 July 1990 were English football's Enlightenment. Not only was this the first time an England team had reached the World Cup semi-final on foreign soil, when for a few precious days we truly *did* believe, but Italia 90 precipitated the birth of a new age for our national game.

From its previous position as a cultural outpost during the 1980s, English football was suddenly positioned at the forefront of social life. Books, television programmes and even theatrical productions with football as their central tenet were all successful. People began to consider football as an art form.

Italia 90 also marked the crossover between football as a working-class game and middle-class pursuit, with satellite television inaugurated and plans for the establishment of the Premier League – for better or for worse – in place. Out of the darkness and into the light (even if that light became too blinding for some).

For those four-and-a-half weeks, a global sporting event played out in glorious technicolour. The green of the grass felt greener, the white of England's shirts seemed brighter than ever before. The television coverage presented Italy with a shimmer and sheen, as it were a month-long dream sequence.

We cried, laughed and sat spellbound as Totò Schillaci ran, Roger Milla danced, Frank Rijkaard spat, Bobby Robson jigged and Gazza cried. Twenty-five thousand hairs on the necks of 25 million people stood on end every time 'Nessun dorma' was played, as if standing to be serenaded by Luciano Pavarotti's majestic version of the aria. England fell to glorious failure, just as they had four years previously, but the emphasis this time was on the glory.

If our eyes were suddenly opened to the possibility of footballing multiculturalism, Italia 90 also re-sold the image of English football and the English football supporter. Papers released in 2012 revealed that the government, still led by Margaret Thatcher, had considered withdrawing the national team from the 1990 World Cup over concerns that it would become a 'natural focus' for hooliganism.

Instead, the travelling hordes proved once and for all that if you treat people as adults, they are far more likely to behave like them. Transport, accommodation and match tickets were available at reasonable prices, a world away from the corporate homogeny that now envelopes each major tournament. There were impromptu kickabouts in town squares, and late-night parties to celebrate good results and forget bad ones. The tournament did not pass without trouble, but the behaviour of England supporters was appreciated by the Italians. A country had prepared for war; it got the odd skirmish.

As Pete Davies, author of the seminal *All Played Out*, told the *Guardian* in 2015: 'Prior to Italia 90, football in England was perceived as a squalid, hooligan-ridden, embarrassing sump of gormless violence. Our team was crap, our supporters were worse, and you did not talk about it over dinner.'

Yet Robson's squad of twenty-two players altered preconceptions. Only two outfielders in the squad were aged thirty or over and, while they limped through the group stages, England were the top scorers in the knockout stages. For the first time in years, our team played with flair *and* solidity, rather than lurching ineffectively between the two. FIFA's technical report on the tournament noted the team's 'ability to adapt and improvise with each other away from their league clubs'. The team having been absent from European competition for five years before the tournament, you can almost detect the surprise in those typed words.

The poster boy for this feelgood wave was Paul Gascoigne, a young Geordie with a glint in his eye and magic in his feet. England's most junior player at Italia 90 was also their best. If an entire country came of age over those thirty-one days, a young central midfielder became a man, and a man became a superstar. Move over Gascoigne; 'Gazza' was born.

What stuck out most about Gascoigne in Robson's team was that he was distinctly continental in style. He was neither England's first flair player nor its first entertainer, but he was our first true street footballer. His technical ability when slaloming past opponents in centre midfield was unsurpassed by any other Englishman of his generation, while his raw natural talent set him apart from almost any other player in world football.

'Mastery of the ball was boring for Gazza,' remembers former Liverpool goalkeeper Ray Clemence. 'Volleying the ball into the net from thirty yards out? He'd do it. Then he'd say, "I know, I'll do it with my eyes closed." He'd do that, too. Then he'd try to find different ways to miskick the ball into the net.'

Already a winner of the PFA Young Player of the Year award after a season that earned him a move from his home-town club Newcastle United to Tottenham, Gascoigne had announced himself as an England star two months before the World Cup against Czechoslovakia at Wembley. He provided three assists in a 4–2 win after England had fallen behind, alleviating concerns that he was a practical joker first and talented footballer second. Had he allowed his devil to take over before the tournament, he may not have made the plane. In Italy, Gascoigne stole the show.

Even twenty-eight years later, there is a hardwired mis-trust of flair and exuberance within some in English football. The British footballing stereotype is that only the hardest will survive, and strength can only be displayed through passionate commitment rather than through skill in the clutch moments. Scratch at the relegation battle in this, last or next season, and you will find managers and pundits demanding that players must show bravery, courage and heart to succeed. That's all true, but courage and exceptional skill need not be mutually exclusive.

This preference for perspiration over inspiration is a throwback to times when football was a sport enjoyed by those who had worked hard all week and wanted to watch others doing the same on a Saturday. But the prolonging of that attitude led to the misuse of some of England's most talented footballers. Glenn Hoddle is surely the best example; Matt Le Tissier is another whose talents merited far greater faith.

Players who had the ability to lift themselves above the rigidity of English football's ethos were viewed negatively. A player who did not run and tackle and fight was viewed as a luxury, whatever their skill level. And luxury was something to be suspicious of, not celebrated. While other countries were building a team around their most skilful players, in England they were marginalised.

Gascoigne was an argument for the opposite strategy, the 'let them play' principle. When a player reaches a higher plane of natural talent, nothing but that talent need matter. And it can prove a benefit to the wider team. As England teammate Peter Beardsley described: 'His enthusiasm was so infectious and the whole squad took so much from him during Italia 90.'

'Gascoigne was a true footballer of the streets – defiant, crafty and intrepid,' says former West Germany international – and then-manager of the national team – Franz Beckenbauer. 'He could cook up ideas you didn't expect.'

That description has suggestions not just of Gascoigne's skill but of his impishness, and that too certainly came to the fore in Italy. There is a magnificent story about Bryan Robson's World Cup ending that Gascoigne recalls in his book *Glorious*.

After England's 0–0 draw with Netherlands on 16 June, their second group-stage game, some of the players sneaked out of their hotel for a few drinks. They eventually ran away from the bar they'd ended up in when they heard sirens and thought that Bobby Robson had sent the police to pick them up, but as they still wanted to carry on the night they went up to Gascoigne's hotel room.

Bryan Robson, England's captain at the tournament, was messing around with Gascoigne and Chris Waddle. Robson was trying to tip a worse-for-wear Gascoigne from his bed and onto the floor when the bed slipped from his grasp and landed on Robson's toe, breaking it. That injury would end Robson's World Cup, with the official announcement made that an old Achilles problem had flared up again.

Less than twelve hours later, and with manager Robson seething about the injury to his namesake, Gascoigne decided to jump as far as he could from the diving board and into the pool. As he did so, he injured his own toe. Gascoigne later admitted that the injury hampered his performances in training. The flaws in Gazza's personality were apparent to every one of his teammates and members of English coaching staff. They just chose to turn a blind eye.

The 1990 World Cup did more than show off the flair of England's players; it exhibited their vulnerabilities too. Before then, the archetypal British footballer was one of two obvious stereotypes. First came the clean-cut local boy made good, with a stiff upper lip in times of crisis and humility when success came his way. Stanley Matthews, Billy Wright, Bobby Charlton and Bobby Moore all fit that image, four players who ran like a seam through five decades of English football.

The alternative was the bulldog, the hard-as-nails defender or midfielder who was prepared to run through walls for his country and then show off the bruises in the bar after the game. The defining image of England's qualification campaign for Italia 90 was not a Gary Lineker goal or piece of John Barnes or Gascoigne skill, but blood pouring from Terry Butcher's head after he received impromptu stitches for a deep cut in the game against Sweden. Having a white shirt stained red was considered a sign of strength at a time when your reputation was directly proportional to the perceived size of your heart.

For either of those stereotypes, crying on the pitch would have been considered extraordinary. Emotion – and certainly over-emotion – was something displayed by our continental cousins, not us. Hard-wired machismo dictated that you had to be tough in order to thrive. To display emotion was to display weakness.

All that changed over the course of three hours on the evening of 4 July in Turin's Stadio delle Alpi. The tears shed by Gascoigne and Stuart Pearce, broadcast to 26.2 million people watching back home, genuinely affected us. We reacted not only on a sporting level, worried that Gascoigne missing the final would hurt England and Pearce's miss would see us eliminated, but on a human, emotional level too. A few months later, Gascoigne would be voted as the BBC's Sports Personality of the Year.

'Normally sportsmen wept because they had just won something or lost something, or perhaps because they were at the end of their career,' Dr Thomas Dixon told the BBC in 2015. Dixon is the author of *Weeping Britannia: Portrait of a Nation in Tears*, and an expert on crying. 'With Gazza it was self-pitying, out of control and in the middle of a match that he should have been trying to win. The thing that was notable was he was running up and down the pitch in tears.'

The unprecedented treatment of a British sportsman crying as something to be cherished rather than mocked was perhaps summed up best by author Salman Rushdie, writing in the *Independent on Sunday*: 'Before Paul Gascoigne, did anyone ever become a national hero and a dead-cert millionaire by crying? Fabulous. Weep and the world weeps with you.'

If Gascoigne's tears had a sporting impact, Dixon believes that this spread to British culture in general. 'It was a very high-profile example of what was by then seen as the culture of the "new man" who shows his feelings,' he says. 'Gascoigne was someone who was a typical man – a "lad", heavy drinking – and it was an example of that meeting the "new man" culture.' Gascoigne had broken down the walls of traditional masculinity.

The peaks and troughs of Gascoigne at that World Cup

were a microcosm of his career and life – a time of great extremes, with adoration by the masses but individual heartache as the denouement.

The dull nature of the tournament football – Italia 90 had the lowest goal-per-game average of any World Cup at 2.21 – allowed for players with flair to shine, and three did so more than most: Roberto Baggio, Robert Prosinečki and Gascoigne. Baggio and Gascoigne were named in FIFA's Team of the Tournament.

Without the eventual lows, the yellow card awarded to Gascoigne by Brazilian referee José Roberto Wright and England's exit, Gascoigne's move to Serie A would probably never have happened. In his book *Glorious*, Gascoigne explains the sense of longing he felt as he walked over to the England supporters after the penalty shootout against Germany:

I looked up and saw the crowd. I burst into tears again. They had come all that way to support us and they were still cheering. I was watching them, thinking, 'How can I ever get back this time again?' I knew I couldn't and I didn't want it to end. I wanted to play football forever that summer. Now it was all over.

The precise nature of Gascoigne's World Cup exit was crucial too, because the dream was shattered in an individual context. Had England gone out on penalties with Gascoigne not carded, he would have been part of a shared experience, a communal grieving. He would have been comforted by colleagues and probably been suitably consoled.

But this was different. England and Gascoigne had risen and fallen over the same few weeks but had separated right at the end. 'He knew the supreme penalty he was going to have to pay for that slight indiscretion,' as Bobby Robson would say.

Although Gascoigne continued to run and pass and dribble after the booking, the grieving process had already started. His tears were the proof of that, fuelling Gascoigne's determination to right the wrong. He had unfinished business.

There is an argument, then, that moving to Serie A was an attempt to prolong that dream period in Gascoigne's professional life, or at least give the dream a different ending before waking up. In Gascoigne's later life, his addictive personality would be laid bare. On some level, the move to Italy was a symptom of that same disease. Gascoigne became addicted to the feelings that Italia 90 provoked within him, and so he chased the dragon.

Whether that is a positive foundation for making a life-changing career decision is open to debate. We can at least be confident that had the World Cup been played in Spain, Mexico, the USA or France, Gascoigne would not have been as keen to move to Serie A.

What's more, the converse is also true. Lazio (and Italians in general) would not have been so enamoured by Gascoigne's move had it not been for his World Cup performances in

Italy. Scouting networks were far less extensive than even a decade later, making Italia 90 – or perhaps USA 94 – the last major tournament in which a player could make a name for themselves in their early twenties.

The Italian public admired Gascoigne's distinctly 'un-English' playing style, his swagger and bravado. But they truly bought into the personality of the boy who wore his heart on his sleeve. Gascoigne's personality had no affectations – what you saw was what you got. In a celebrity culture where falseness was rife, Italian supporters found |that transparency incredibly endearing.

Crucially, Gascoigne had also demonstrated that he was incredibly popular with the public. As the crowds gathered at Heathrow to welcome home Robson's team, they clamoured not after top scorer Lineker or stand-in captain Butcher, but after Gascoigne.

As Simon Kuper wrote in his book *Football Against the Enemy*, Gascoigne's reputation as a majestic footballer was established before the World Cup, but the semi-final in Turin gave birth to Gazzamania, for better and for worse.

In the months following Italia 90, Gascoigne had his waxwork installed in London's Madame Tussauds, turned on the Christmas lights on Regent Street, was introduced on his television show by Terry Wogan as 'the most famous and probably the most popular man in Britain today', was described by his legal counsel as more famous than the Duke of Wellington and released two singles in the space of a month. The 'distinctive' 'Fog on the Tyne', a remake of the

1971 album title track by English folk rock band Lindis-farne, failed to meet the expectation that it would top the charts. The cover of the single, picturing Gascoigne wearing headphones while singing into a microphone, depicted a man desperately out of his comfort zone. The second, 'Geordie Boys (Gazza Rap)', was as unsuccessful as its musical merits deserved.

As former Manchester United manager and pundit Tommy Docherty said with tragic prophecy: 'The poor boy is a talented enough footballer, sure, but he is in mighty danger of becoming nothing more than the fairy on top of the Christmas tree.'

For Serie A, a league already boasting the reputation of being the strongest in world football, Gazzamania made Gascoigne a marketer's dream. He was placed fourth in the Ballon d'Or voting in 1990, with the other four members of the top five (Lothar Matthäus, Salvatore Schillaci, Andreas Brehme and Franco Baresi) all based in Italy. Of the rest of the top ten, three (Jürgen Klinsmann, Roberto Baggio and Frank Rijkaard) were already playing in Serie A, while Enzo Scifo joined Torino in 1991. If Gascoigne was going to move abroad, Italy was the natural destination.

Gascoigne's then-personal assistant Jane Nottage – who would go on to write a warts-and-all book on his time on Italy (Gascoigne reacted badly to its publication and disputed information contained within) – described meeting with Serie A officials keen to recruit players from the English First Division to Italy with football journalist Jeff Powell.

The Italians were eager to determine which players the pair felt would be most marketable, but Nottage's presence (and association with Gascoigne) indicates that he was at the top of their list.

The three players discussed – Gascoigne, Des Walker and David Platt – would all join Italian clubs, but Gascoigne was comfortably the most marketable. He was the everyman who could be moulded into the superstar, whatever that might mean for him personally.

Gascoigne would never play in another World Cup. England failed him in 1994 and Glenn Hoddle failed him in 1998. But in the space of three weeks, Gascoigne had established the frenzy that would define both his next career move and the rest of his professional life.

'Gascoigne has the world at his feet,' as the *Independent* headline read two days after defeat to Germany, when the wheels were already in motion for his next step. England's exit and Gascoigne's tears had precipitated not a witch-hunt but a baptism. If Gazzamania craved an environment in which it could be magnified, Rome was a better location than most.

INGRESSO
NELLA CAPITALE

Knee troubles, the transfer
saga and the arrival
in Rome

In 1991 Tottenham Hotspur were deep in the throes of financial austerity. Chairman Irving Scholar had floated the club on the stock exchange in 1983, the first club in the world to be publicly listed, turning Spurs from being a sporting institution into a commercial entity, where they would diversify into leisure wear and computer systems.

Scholar set a trend that would eventually become the norm, but Tottenham soon ran into trouble. The diversification of business interests was supplemented by investment in new players, including the arrival of Gascoigne himself in 1988 from Newcastle United, and the building of a new stand at White Hart Lane. The club soon had mounting debts and unhappy lenders.

Scholar turned to media mogul Robert Maxwell, who secretly lent him £1.1m, but when Scholar's business partner Paul Bobroff discovered this the pair fell out. That left manager Terry Venables to search for backers to save the club from financial ruin, eventually leading to Alan Sugar's involvement. Sugar had been taken to White Hart Lane as a child, although he had not shown a particularly keen interest in the club or football as a whole. Sugar did the deal, made himself chairman and banned Scholar from the club.

Sugar was not a strong argument for nominative determinism; he was a businessman not a sugar-daddy, and viewed Tottenham as an asset rather than a cherished possession. When Tottenham's finances were examined in great detail, the new chairman realised that players would have to be sold to wipe out debts. The newly established Gazzamania ensured that Gascoigne was the most obvious star departure.

In her book *Paul Gascoigne: The Inside Story*, Nottage claims that she received a call to inform her that football agent Dennis Roach had been instructed by Tottenham to try to sell Gascoigne to a Serie A club after they had been put under pressure by the banks to raise capital.

Gascoigne himself says that he first heard of a potential move in February 1991, when rumours surfaced that Lazio wanted him. He was upset not at the interest from abroad, but that Tottenham had been discussing his exit without thinking to inform the player first, as if he was a product to be sold rather than a person. Gascoigne recalls feeling incredibly let down by Tottenham's behaviour, which clearly made the move away from White Hart Lane more attractive.

With Italy the obvious destination and the World Cup still fresh in the memory, AC Milan and Lazio both made approaches to Tottenham, although Lazio's was far more concrete. But Gascoigne could easily have joined Juventus had things turned out differently.

After the third-place play-off at Italia 90, Gianni Agnelli, head of Fiat and key advisor (with far more influence than that implies) to Juventus, having run the club himself between

1947 and 1954, walked into the England dressing room and asked to speak to Gascoigne. The story goes that Gascoigne grabbed Agnelli in a boisterous headlock and slapped his head. Were it anyone else, we would assume exaggeration or apocrypha; but this was Gascoigne. We can assume that Agnelli was not accustomed to such treatment, and certainly not by someone who he had never previously met. Either way, the deal was never likely from that point on.

Lazio soon became the frontrunners for a deal. President Gianmarco Calleri had become transfixed with the idea of signing Gascoigne after witnessing his popularity during the World Cup, believing him the perfect signing to improve the club on and off the field, and general manager Maurizio Manzini was on board. There was also a story that Gianmarco's brother Giorgio, who would soon pass away, was desperate for Lazio to sign Gascoigne. After Giorgio's death, Gianmarco was eager to carry out his brother's wishes.

Tottenham initially asked for £10m from Lazio, which made an opening offer of half that amount. A fee of £7.5m was eventually thrashed out, with an agreement that Gascoigne would be paraded around the Stadio Olimpico before Lazio's final home league game of the 1990/91 season. That took place a week after the FA Cup Final.

Meanwhile, Mel Stein and Len Lazarus – Gascoigne's two personal advisors – thrashed out the terms of Gascoigne's contract. Lazio's new signing would be paid £22,000 a week in Italy, ten times his wage at Tottenham. The star of English football was moving to Italy.

Tottenham supporters soon got wind of the interest from Lazio when stories were leaked to Italian newspapers. Their immediate reaction was to criticise Gascoigne for a perceived lack of loyalty, but that is understandable. Disloyalty or greed on the part of a player is a far more palatable – and perhaps even typical – scenario than the club being forced to hawk out its best players to raise money to stave off bankruptcy.

On the pitch, Tottenham were progressing well in the FA Cup, with Gascoigne the star. He had scored twice against Oxford United in the fourth round and scored two more against Portsmouth in the fifth. A quarter-final victory over Notts County set up a north London derby semi-final at Wembley against Arsenal, with Gascoigne playing after eight injections for a hernia injury that would subsequently require surgery.

All the while, rumours of negotiations with Lazio were being leaked in the dressing room, although Gascoigne was proving to his teammates and manager Terry Venables that the distractions would not affect his game. Even the hernia operation would not push him off course. He was ready for Arsenal.

Before the semi-final, Venables recalls how Gascoigne was more hyped up and tense than he had ever seen him before, as if desperate to prove that he merited the lucrative move that would soon be announced. That afternoon, Gascoigne produced one of the most memorable Wembley performances and one of the most memorable FA Cup goals.

His free-kick is extraordinary. Rather than running from the side to impart curl on the ball, as is standard, Gascoigne runs from straight on, preferring power. The ball rises from the moment it leaves his foot and continues on that trajectory until it eventually connects with the top corner of David Seaman's net less than a second later. There is no arc on the ball, as you might expect, just a straight-line path. The power on the shot almost sent the ball back out of the goal.

The masterly Barry Davies said it best on commentary: 'Oh, I say. Brilliant! That. Is. Schoolboy's own stuff. Oh! I bet even he can't believe it. Is there anything left from this man to surprise us? That was one of the finest free-kicks that this stadium has ever seen. Seaman got his hands, couldn't hold. Spurs have the lead. Paul Gascoigne, the scorer.'

Gascoigne's brilliance in that semi-final, despite being super-charged before the game, is important, because it reflects his unpredictability as a personality. When Venables saw his prodigy in a similar state ahead of the final in the same stadium, he figured that he would get the same reaction. Although the Spurs manager would later be criticised for not leaving Gascoigne out of the side, it's worth considering what the backlash might have been had Tottenham lost the game, particularly given the rumours of a move. Supporters would have believed that Tottenham's financial welfare was being protected over competitive interest and glory.

There is also something in a quote from Gascoigne given to the BBC in 2011 to indicate why he was quite so riled for that final: 'If ever I got man of the match, the next game

I would tell myself that I had to get man of the match and score. If I scored a couple, the next game I had to get three. That was the way I was.'

Having scored a wonderful free-kick and being the best player in the semi-final, Gascoigne reasoned that he had to improve upon that against Nottingham Forest or disappoint. It is a flawed, and slightly childlike, take, but then that was Gascoigne. The constant pursuit of greater and greater returns will test the resolve of even the strongest mentality. He could never boast that.

Gascoigne recalls the Tottenham club doctor being sent to the hotel room, where Gascoigne was kicking pillows and volleying bars of soap, to give him some tablets to calm him down. We can assume that these were Valium. When he was manic again before kick-off, Venables sat him down and tried to get him to breathe deeply and relax.

Gascoigne himself says it was merely the pressure to show that he merited all the praise and mania that provoked his FA Cup Final actions. He wanted to prove the Tottenham supporters who believed him to be a mercenary wrong, and he wanted to make his family – who were in attendance – proud. This was also his chance to say a fitting goodbye to English football on the biggest stage. He had bought dozens of tickets at Wembley for his friends from the north-east.

'I was loving the hype but people didn't realise it can get quite scary,' Gascoigne later recalled. 'There were people carrying cardboard cutouts, old women telling me what I should do, and three-year-olds looking at me and saying, "Mum, that's Gazza." I thought "Whoa."'

At that point, the deal to take Gascoigne to Lazio had been agreed, but only verbally. Gascoigne had not signed a contract because he wanted to go into the final with the mindset that he was still fully a Tottenham player.

Within minutes of the start of the game, Gascoigne should have been sent off for a wild, high challenge on Forest's Garry Parker, planting a boot into Parker's midriff but only being penalised with a free-kick.

'I wish I'd got sent off for the first tackle on Parker,' Gascoigne later said to the BBC. 'I remember he'd clattered me in one game but I waited two years to get him back. He was one of their playmakers and what you try to do is injure his legs. If you're going to challenge him, make sure he can't kick a ball as well as he can if you hurt his feet or legs. But I nearly took his windpipe out.'

Ten minutes later came the moment that left an indelible mark on Gascoigne's career, as he tried to leave an indelible mark on Gary Charles's shin. The tackle was wincingly wild and tempestuous, like an angry child kicking down his younger sibling's snowman out of spite. Charles was incredibly fortunate to get to his feet unscathed, but Gascoigne required a minute of treatment before taking his place in the defensive wall.

As Stuart Pearce's free-kick flew past Erik Thorstvedt into the same Wembley goal where Gascoigne had scored so famously weeks before, the Tottenham star was slumping to the ground in pain. He had ruptured his cruciate knee ligament.

With Lazio officials in the crowd to witness their impending arrival during his English football swansong, Gascoigne was rushed into an ambulance and to the Princess Grace Hospital in central London. Not only was he concerned that he had let down his teammates – he was obviously fearful that he had ruined his chance of a move abroad.

It was to their credit (and a testament to Lazio's determination to sign the player) that general manager Manzini and sporting director Carlo Regalia soon visited Gascoigne in hospital, taking him a Lazio shirt and a gold watch as a gesture of their commitment to the transfer and their relationship. With the media in England and Italy both reporting that the injury could put the move in jeopardy, it was just the comfort Gascoigne needed at a difficult time.

But despite Lazio's commitment to Gascoigne, it was clear that the severity of the injury would trigger a renegotiation on the price, with Tottenham hardly in a position of strength to reject whatever Lazio offered. Rather than having Sugar, whom Venables was already beginning to mistrust, take part in the negotiations, the Tottenham manager instead used Gino Santin, an Italian based in London. Santin was not particularly accomplished by all accounts, but a compromise was reached. Lazio had originally proposed that the fee would be reduced to £4.7m, but Tottenham haggled to a £5.5m sum that would eventually increase to £6.2m with add-ons. The Premier League would in time decide that

Santin's third-party involvement was a breach of Football Association rules.

The Wembley injury would not be the only complication in Gascoigne's Italian move. A few months into his recovery, Gascoigne interrupted a bar fight in which his sister Lindsay had been assaulted and punched a man to the floor. Gascoigne actually hit the wrong man, and was arrested and charged with assault.

The differing reactions to the incident in the English and Italian media helped to convince Gascoigne that he would enjoy life in Serie A. The English press were keen to sell the fracas as another example of Gascoigne's yobbishness and alcohol-fuelled problems. The Italian media, pandering to a very different culture, portrayed Gascoigne as the knight in shining armour rushing to defend his sister in distress. The duty of an elder brother to protect the honour of his younger sister is well established in Italian society.

Far worse was to come in September 1991. A few weeks previously, and with his recuperation slightly ahead of schedule thanks to his one-on-one work with Tottenham physio John Sheridan, Gascoigne had journeyed to Rome to be introduced to the club's supporters. While there, he witnessed the power of Gazzamania first-hand.

The airport and press conference were packed, despite the renegotiations for the move still not being finalised. For his part, Gascoigne played his role as Gazza perfectly, cracking jokes and talking up his commitment to getting fit and playing for Lazio. He was introduced to his new teammates at the Stadio Olimpico before being paraded to the fans in the stadium while 'Fog on the Tyne' played to the crowd. As Gascoigne remembers fondly in his autobiography, a banner was displayed in the stands: 'Gazza's men are here, shag women and drink beer'. It's nice to feel appreciated.

This was Lazio's demonstrative gesture that they were committed to providing Gascoigne with a new home, but it also showed Gascoigne's commitment to the club and its supporters, and that his career-threatening injury had not dissuaded him from the move. Upon his return to England, he prepared to say his last goodbyes.

Part of those goodbyes involved him travelling from London to the north-east to bid farewell to his old friends in Dunston, the part of Gateshead where he was born. One evening, he was out drinking with friends and they went into a nightclub. A man he did not know approached him and, blindsiding him, punched him to the floor. The injury was not caused by the punch, but by Gascoigne's leg giving way again as he fell to the ground. All the work of the surgeons, and all the physio and recuperative exercises was immediately undone. Although the cruciate itself was not damaged, Gascoigne's kneecap had been broken and displaced.

The second injury floored Gascoigne – literally and mentally. Once is never but twice is always, and Gascoigne believed, perfectly reasonably, that not just his Lazio move but his entire career was in serious jeopardy. The phrase used in his autobiography is typically candid, but highly appropriate: 'After all that work. I thought, fuck it.'

There was also far less sympathy for Gascoigne both inside and outside the game this time, given the circumstances of his injury. The challenge on Charles was reckless, but at least it took place within the confines of a football pitch. Any player who suffers self-inflicted distress when in a social – rather than professional – situation is likely to be scalded for their treatment, and the media reasoned that Gascoigne had form. Tottenham chairman Sugar was reportedly furious that the move might again be in doubt.

And yet it's entirely unfair to blame Gascoigne for this second knee injury. Being out in a nightclub as a footballer in the early 1990s was closer to the rule than the exception, and English football was still locked in a culture of casual – and non-casual – drinking that allowed dependency to fester. It was not until the arrival of Arsène Wenger at Arsenal in 1996 that the drinking culture was eliminated and the concepts of nutrition and wellness introduced.

Gascoigne was also an honest, working-class lad, deeply loyal. It would break a part of him to lose contact with his old friends, and it never occurred to him to avoid meeting them to say goodbye. Take his mates away from him, and you took away a part of the man – and thus part of the player too. Gascoigne was simply in the wrong place at the wrong time, confronted by the wrong man.

Yet Gascoigne did not let repeated disaster defeat him. He was entirely committed to his new programme of recovery and jumped through every one of the hoops that Lazio demanded in order to pass their medical tests. He even arranged an extra training session with a group of Tottenham youth-team players to impress the visiting Manzini, doubly proving his physical strength. Eventually a date of 31 May 1992 was agreed for Gascoigne's transfer, almost a year after the initial completion date.

If the obvious question is why Lazio stayed so committed to a transfer and player who gave them nothing but headaches, the club's change in ownership structure in 1992 provides a part-explanation.

In 1991 businessman Sergio Cragnotti had been encouraged by his brother to move into the world of football club ownership. Cragnotti was the head of Italian food conglomerate Cirio, and was seen at the Stadio Olimpico in March 1991 when Lazio beat Juventus 1–0. He came from a family of Lazio supporters, and was persuaded to make an offer to Gianmarco Calleri.

When the purchase was eventually completed in March 1992, Gascoigne was close to recovery following his injury setback. Cragnotti had lofty aims for Lazio, planning to take them far above their traditional status as also-rans. While Calleri would have been blowing the budget on Gascoigne, Cragnotti viewed him as a necessary statement signing and one that he could readily afford.

Calleri had signed one major non-Italian player in each previous season (Rubén Sosa in 1988/89, Pedro Troglio in 1989/90, Karl-Heinz Riedle in 1990/91 and Thomas Doll in 1991/92), but Cragnotti was far less circumspect in his investment in domestic and foreign players, despite

Serie A enforcing a policy of allowing only three for-
eigners in a matchday squad for domestic league and cup
matches.

Gascoigne was joined in 1992 by Aron Winter from Ajax,
Diego Fuser from Inter and Giuseppe Signori from Foggia,
and the following season Alen Bokšić would join from
Marseille, Luca Marchegiani from Torino, Pierluigi Casiraghi
from Juventus, José Chamot from Foggia and Roberto Di
Matteo from FC Aarau for combined transfer fees of close
to £20m.

The reason that Lazio had never before spent freely is
that it had never before been consistently successful. It had
won the Scudetto in 1973/74, largely thanks to the goals of
Giorgio Chinaglia, but in the four seasons before Gascoigne's
arrival had finished 10th, 9th, 11th and 10th. Lazio had
been in Serie B as recently as 1988 and hadn't finished in
Serie A's top six since 1977. Cragnotti's lavish spending
would instigate the most successful period in the club's history. At £5.5m, Gascoigne was the message sent to the rest
of Europe that Cragnotti intended to turn Lazio into a
European superpower.

The other pertinent question is whether the two injuries
changed Gascoigne. He remains adamant that they didn't,
rightly pointing out that he still reached significant on-
pitch highs with club and country following his double
recovery. But Gascoigne also describes getting a kick on his
competitive Lazio debut and being unsure after getting back
to his feet whether his knee would hold up when making the

next pass. How long into his time in Italy did these doubts – even subconsciously – last?

There is also the evidence from Gascoigne's physio John Sheridan, who described the extent of Gascoigne's initial injury:

It is to Gazza's great credit that he has played again. His was one of the worst injuries I have had to work on, and some footballers wouldn't have kicked a ball again. The fact that he is playing again is down to several things, the most important being his love of football and his dedication to getting fit.

Given Sheridan's assessment, Gascoigne's career from this point deserves to be judged in a favourable light. If the wheels of his move to Italy had not already been set in motion before the FA Cup Final, it seems highly unlikely that it would have happened at all, and so Gascoigne warrants praise that he twice worked back from such severe adversity to make it happen. Staying in England would have been the easier way out.

Whether it was the right move at the right time is open to debate. There is certainly an argument that Gascoigne would have been better recovering from such an extended spell away from the game far from the bubble of Italian football in a more relaxed environment. Nothing had prepared Gascoigne for the furore that would welcome him upon his eventual arrival in Rome, where Gazzamania had proliferated during the desperate wait.

But that was never Gascoigne's style. He was a player for whom mania was a natural state, who would have created his own had it not naturally existed. Ironically, the only climate in which he could operate successfully was also the one in which he struggled to cope. Welcome to Italian football. Welcome to Rome. Welcome to mania.

LE PRIME PENNELLATE

The genius at work,
first-season blossoming

Gascoigne has always been aware of his audience and keen to play up to his reputation in order to sustain it. This is never done with any degree of calculation – in fact, closer to the opposite. He is a man who wants desperately to be loved. As a player, he found love particularly easy to come by simply by being – as Bobby Robson called him – 'daft as a brush', a phrase that was used by Gascoigne as the title of an offbeat autobiographical book published in 1989.

In Rome, Gascoigne began in full charm-offensive mode – or at least his version of the strategy. He turned up at his first press conference wearing a pair of joke glasses and a flat cap emblazoned with the logo of the *Irriducibili*, Lazio's ultra supporters. His first fortnight in Italy was spent cheerleading, talking up his appetite for his new life.

This approach extended to his new teammates, who were aware of the frenzy surrounding Gascoigne but cannot have been prepared for the eccentricity of his arrival. Before his first day of training, Gascoigne visited a bookshop in the city and bought twenty copies of a language guide for Italians learning English. A copy of the book was placed on the designated benches in the dressing room at the training ground as a welcome message to each player. If their amused reaction was predictable, so is the story that Gascoigne forgot his boots for that initial session, and so turned up to his first training session wearing plimsolls.

Lazio's priority was to settle Gascoigne in Rome. They put him in a villa in Formello, a suburb twelve miles from the city centre, and made two crucial gestures to ensure that the potentially difficult acclimatisation process would be as smooth as possible. The first was to play a two-legged friendly with his former club Tottenham, branded as the Capital Cup (between teams in the capital cities of England and Italy), which would give Gascoigne a chance to gain match fitness having missed the start of the season. The gate receipts from the two games would go to Tottenham, negotiated as part of the transfer.

It also gave the Lazio supporters an opportunity to see their new midfielder in action for the first time, and an un-precedented 30,000 turned up for what was a non-competitive game. As if to show his appreciation for their support during the drawn-out saga of his transfer, Gascoigne scored in the first leg in the Stadio Olimpico and jumped over the advertising hoardings behind the goal to salute his audience.

In the return fixture at White Hart Lane, Gascoigne appreciated the overwhelming support of the home crowd for their returning player. He had been concerned in the build-up to the game that he might be subject to catcalls about his departure and accusations of greed. Gascoigne was perennially worried about what people thought of him, but his reception that evening felt to him as though he was being given the blessing of the English football public. Any unease he had about starting a new life in Italy evaporated.

The second gesture from Lazio was to bestow on Gascoigne their No. 10 shirt, the importance of which cannot be overstated. In England, shirt numbers have symbolic meaning at certain clubs – No. 7 at Manchester United and Liverpool, No. 9 at Newcastle United, No. 6 at West Ham – but this is typically due to the success of previous wearers of the shirt. No number on its own truly holds any value as a cultural entity.

In Italy – as elsewhere in world football – the No. 10 shirt has a revered significance. In an era before squad numbers, No. 10s were players who controlled attacks with their vision, skill and creativity, with either dribbling or passing as an extra-special power. More importantly still, players were bred to play this position from a young age, and so continental teams became defined by their No. 10s.

In Italy, No. 10s are respected perhaps more than anywhere else in the world (although Argentina may have a strong case) and are known as *fantasisti*. It is no coincidence that Italy is the only country where the No. 10 shirt has been retired by more than one high-ranking club – Brescia (for Roberto Baggio) and Napoli (for Diego Maradona). It was rumoured that Roma would do the same for Francesco Totti, but that idea appears to have been shelved.

The extra significance of this attacking playmaker in Italian football comes as a result of the traditional *catenaccio* style that came to define their game and which still acts as a stereotype for Serie A today. *Fantasisti* who could rise above the rigidity, physicality and defensiveness of the game were cherished both as likely match-winners and as entertainers. In *Calcio*, his seminal book on Italian football, John Foot picks out five *fantasisti*: Mario Corso, Gigi Meroni, Roberto Baggio, Gianfranco Zola and Totti. Add in the great Giancarlo Antognoni of Fiorentina, and you have a seam that runs unbroken through sixty years of Italian football.

For Gascoigne to be bestowed with the No. 10 shirt as an Englishman was clearly an honour for him, but also reflects the impression that he made within England's team at Italia 90. The English game had long been renowned for deliberately producing powerful footballers over technical ones, with the European ban in the 1980s blamed for making English football even more insular. Gascoigne, like Glenn Hoddle before him, bucked that trend and took his wares to Europe.

Having proved his fitness against Spurs, Gascoigne made his Serie A debut against Genoa on 27 September. Lazio billed it as Speciale Gazza Day, creating an extra fanfare around their star man. Fans wearing T-shirts that bore the messages 'God Save Gazza' and 'Gazza the Giant' gathered in the garden of Gascoigne's villa to wish him well, and he was serenaded by choruses of 'Paul Gascoigne la-la-la-la-la' to the tune of Boney M's 'Brown Girl in the Ring'.

Gascoigne's competitive debut was his career in Italy in microcosm. There were sublime moments to make the 50,000 fans in the Stadio Olimpico scream his name, but the threat of physical injury loomed around every corner. He glided past Genoa's Andrea Fortunato and Cláudio Branco in one move within the first twenty minutes and demonstrated his natural eye for the right run, repeatedly finding space in the penalty area.

But after forty minutes Mario Bortolazzi's stern challenge sent Gascoigne sprawling to the floor, with Lazio's medics sprinting faster than any player on the pitch and an entire stadium waiting for news like a family cooped up in a hospital waiting room. Gascoigne would take to his feet, limp around for a few minutes until half-time and then be substituted by manager Dino Zoff.

The injury was not serious – Gascoigne basically had a dead leg and Zoff was planning to bring him off early in any case – but it was instructive that one strong, mistimed tackle caused so much angst. As Gascoigne himself wrote in *Glorious*, 'I really thought that was going to be the end of my career.' Imagine the emotional stress of considering this as a possible end result every time you took to the field.

Gascoigne's first season in Italy was by far his most successful. He would start twenty-two league games and complete ninety minutes in twelve of them, with only nine of his teammates managing more than his 1,696 Serie A minutes.

It is hardly any surprise that the problems that did surface in 1992/93 were due to injury issues. Gascoigne had had sixteen months out of the game prior to his Lazio debut, and soft-tissue injuries are almost inevitable after such a lay-off, particularly given the rudimentary methods of football physiotherapy at the time. Gascoigne then broke his cheek-bone after being elbowed by Holland's Jan Wouters in a World Cup qualifier in April 1993, and wore a *Phantom of the Opera*-style mask in order to play out the remainder of the season at club level.

Lazio certainly succeeded that season. They finished fifth in Serie A, their highest position since 1975. In a tight league (only nine points separated relegated Fiorentina and Juventus in fourth), Lazio's home form earned them qualification for European competition for the first time since 1978. They only lost twice in the Stadio Olimpico all season in all competitions, had victories over third-placed Parma (5–2), second-placed Inter (3–1) and a 2–2 draw with champions and European Cup finalists Milan, with Gascoigne start-ing two of these three games, scoring against Milan and being given a standing ovation when substituted against Parma.

There are two moments of brilliance that truly stand out in Gascoigne's debut campaign, and they came within eight days of each other. In late November 1992 Lazio were stuck in a rut. They had won just two of their opening ten games in Serie A, and were humbled by Milan at the San Siro in a game that Gascoigne described as an eye-opener for just how far ahead of Lazio Fabio Capello's team were. The Milan team that won that game 5–3 were not the best XI in Italian football history (that honour surely goes to the 1989/90 side), but were still breathtaking: Rossi, Maldini, Tassotti,

Costacurta, Baresi, Donadoni, Albertini, Gullit, van Basten, Lentini, Papin.

Lazio followed up that defeat with a home victory over Atalanta, but then lost to Torino and Foggia. As they entered the Derby della Capitale on 28 November, Lazio were in the bottom half of Serie A, the only positive spin for Cragnotti being that Roma were one point and three places below them.

Even that gap looked in doubt when Lazio were trailing 1–0 with five minutes of the derby remaining. Gascoigne had been shocked by the intensity of the build-up to the match, with thousands of Lazio fans watching training each day, and was surprised again when he saw the gigantic tifos in each end of the ground.

'They never stop talking about it, all day and all night wherever I go. I'm finding it hard, so I've just sat in the house for a week,' Gascoigne said in an interview two days before the game. 'If I go out, people are beeping their horns and stopping me and telling me we have to win. This Sunday is like life or death. Hopefully after Sunday I'm still alive.' Gascoigne would eventually say that the Derby della Capitale even put the Old Firm game into the shade when it came to intensity and atmosphere.

It was a surprise that Gascoigne was on the pitch at all with so little of the game remaining, but when Lazio won a free-kick forty yards from goal, he was the obvious candidate to take it. Gascoigne remembers Signori taking the ball off him and explaining that he was so poor at heading that

Gascoigne would be better served being in the penalty area.

Signori's free-kick was pretty poor, floated into the penalty area rather than whipped in. Gascoigne's assessment that he 'put a strong neck on it' does himself a grave disservice, because the power he generated through a ball that was behind him was extraordinary. From a standing jump, his header was too powerful for Roma's Giuseppe Zinetti to even dive.

Gascoigne had his first Lazio goal, and celebrated as if he were standing on the Stadio Olimpico's Curva Nord. He flung himself over the advertising hoardings, took several paces onto the running track and then stood, arms aloft and leaning backward as if physically held back by the sheer weight of noise.

Earlier in the game, Gascoigne had been the target of jibes about his weight. Roma fans held a banner that read 'Paul Gascoigne, You Are Big Poofter', and threw Mars bars at him. Gascoigne picked one of them up, tore off the wrapper and took a large bite. You could always rely on Gascoigne to play the moment rather than the long game, even if that meant consuming a chocolate bar midway through an athletic contest.

Now the Roma fans were silent as Gascoigne's name reverberated around the stadium. Lazio fans had their hero.

If that goal ensured Gascoigne's cult-hero status, his goal against Pescara in the next game demonstrated the man's truly exceptional natural talents, which must never be clouded by the noise surrounding his personality and his mental health issues. He was, to quote Gary Lineker, 'the most naturally gifted footballer England has ever produced'; according to Sir Alex Ferguson, he was simply 'the best player of his era'.

Gascoigne's dribbling ability was the stuff of comic-book heroes, his burst into space, drop of the shoulder and swagger distinctly un-English. But he also had a coolness in front of goal, a capacity to disguise where he was shooting or passing that made every one of his moments on the ball eminently watchable. You didn't know what Gazza would do next, but you knew it would be good.

Importantly, there was also a rawness to Gascoigne's play that was immensely endearing. Sometimes, the most naturally gifted players appear divine, because it becomes obvious very quickly that you could never hope to replicate their skills. While that was certainly true of Gascoigne when he glided past opponents, you could see the cogs turning as he jinked and surged forward with the ball. Put simply, Gascoigne was the type of footballer you'd pay to watch warm up with a tennis ball.

A dribble is usually most effective when performed at pace, because pace narrows the opponent's margin for error. Commit too early and the protagonist can easily shift to the side and continue on their merry way. Commit too late and the best the opponent can hope to do is foul the dribbler. Think Lionel Messi.

Gascoigne's knack – and one shared by the great Michael Laudrup in La Liga at the same time – was to slow down the dribble and beat the opponent not with pace and athleticism, but with pure technique. Dribbling below sprinting speed requires more touches of the ball, more visual perception of where the next opponent might come from and greater control. Both methods are spectacular (and this is not an attempt to rank one over the other), but neither Gascoigne nor Laudrup had sufficient pace to rely upon that as an effective weapon. This was all about skill.

Finally, like all the best dribblers, Gascoigne gave his opponent a chance. Or, to be more accurate, he made his opponent believe that he had a chance. Like a matador with a bull, a magician with a trick or a comedian with a perfectly timed joke, Gascoigne would play with an opponent's expectations. He would nudge the ball just far enough away from his body to force a defender into committing himself to a challenge. The exact moment that the challenge game, Gascoigne would touch the ball away. You thought you were in control of the situation; you never were.

Some successful attacking midfielders do that twice a match. Gascoigne could do it twice in the space of three seconds. As one particularly flamboyant Italian journalist put it: 'This unconstrained lunatic Gascoigne has exhumed an ancient muscle movement which has the rare beauty of a valuable relic.'

All that beauty was displayed against Pescara when, midway through the first half with the score at 0–0, Gascoigne picked up the ball forty yards from goal. He beat his first two opponents with the same move, a surge of speed from a standing start that made both players (including future World Cup-winning captain Dunga) look as if they were standing in quick-drying cement.

That first move also demonstrated an easily overlooked part of Gascoigne's game. If his susceptibility to injury suggests that he was in some way frail or fair-weather, nothing could be further from the truth. Gascoigne's unusual flair made him a target for physical treatment, and he quickly learned to take a kick, ride challenges and still stay on his feet. So when he was tackled with both a shoulder barge and attempted trip, Gascoigne was knocked off balance but not toppled over.

Next came an opponent who was made to look a fool, committing far too early to the challenge and making connection only with thin air and grass. By the time he had turned his head to see if Gascoigne had been pushed off course, another teammate had made exactly the same mistake. This time contact was made with Gascoigne's shin, but still he ran on.

It is at this point that it's easy to believe fate takes over. When watching all the great individual goals – Maradona vs England, Messi vs Getafe, Giggs vs Arsenal – there is a stage where you refuse to believe the dribbler can be stopped. It is as if we have entered a computer-game world; beating three opponents affords the character a period of invincibility. Nothing the defender now does can matter.

This is not just mere whimsy; it has a basis in reality. Elite sportspeople often talk about being 'in the zone', a higher state of being where their already highly honed abilities are at their peak for a short period of time. When these athletes are pushed to their absolute limits, they enter a psychological state – often entirely subconsciously – in which instinct and practised ability take over. They speak anecdotally about time slowing down to enable them to make informed decisions about their movements under less pressure than is usual. It's hardly surprising that such athletes attribute an ethereal quality to this state of mind.

Gascoigne is now in the zone. When a Pescara defender leaves the ground to throw himself into a challenge, Lazio's No. 10 jumps over his leg as if he were skipping with joy. He has arrived in the penalty area and, having made five outfield players look foolish, it is time for goalkeeper Fabio Marchioro to suffer the same fate.

Now is the moment for Gascoigne to show off his other great skill: he is almost equally comfortable with his left and right foot. Marchioro comes out of his goal, and immediately makes a move to his left. Given that Gascoigne is right-footed, that makes sense. Attackers are taught that their best chance of scoring is to shoot across the goalkeeper, and Marchioro would have expected Gascoigne to bring the ball onto his right foot, open up his body and attempt to slot the ball around the goalkeeper's grasp with his right instep, using the natural curl on the ball to bring it back towards goal.

Gascoigne being Gascoigne has other ideas. Watching the goal again, you can see his half-second shimmy. That shimmy wrong-foots Marchioro, but also allows Gascoigne to open up his body for a left-footed shot. With the goalkeeper pushing his weight the wrong way, Gascoigne can aim for the near corner and make the dive look amateur.

In the space of six seconds, Gascoigne has beaten more than half of the Pescara team in an individual battle. He runs to the corner where Lazio's sparse away support is standing, and fans battle to sprint down to the lower tier and salute their new king. Most are left literally jumping for joy, captivated by what they have witnessed. It is surely the best goal of Gascoigne's career.

IL DIVO

*The clown prince, the
people's favourite*

It was never in doubt that Gascoigne would be a hit in Rome, for he was popular wherever he laid his hat. The boast that he was the reason for Lazio's attendances rising by between 5,000 and 10,000 in his first season would seem doubtful given that Lazio as a whole improved significantly on the pitch, but president Cragnotti was in no doubt. 'He added 10,000 to our season-ticket sales, and he has established himself immediately as our fans' hero. That was instantaneous,' he told the *Independent* in 1992. Gazzamania certainly survived the thousand-mile journey from London.

There is no secret recipe for a footballer to secure cult-hero status. Supporters want to feel close to players and develop an affinity with them through shared experience. That might stem from a player's place of birth, upbringing or family history, but with Gascoigne in Rome it came purely through the warmth of his personality.

Gascoigne was the archetypal cult hero. He was fun-loving and crazy, as is every loyal Italian football fan, but he balanced that with a demonstrative respect for their worship of the team. Lazio fan Luca Pasqualini said exactly that to *FourFourTwo* magazine in 2017:

It was obvious from the start that he was different from the others: he was a man, a friend, a joker, but above all a player who respected the Lazio shirt, something a lot of people forget today. He always had a lot in common with the supporters: the respect, the will, the passion and the fantasy. There was a time when Gazza, Lazio and the fans were the same thing.

But cult-hero status often begins far earlier than the start of a player's professional career. It has roots in football's role in childhood, and therefore what becoming a star player means to the individual. It is something that cannot be manufactured, but grows organically.

'I started off with a tennis ball; I took it everywhere,' Gascoigne once told *Shortlist* magazine. 'Then, when I was seven, my dad came back from working as a hod-carrier in Germany and brought me a football. I kicked that thing for hours and hours. I was obsessed. It seemed to stick to my feet. I was eight and playing against twelve-year-olds and seemed to be beating them for fun.'

This is a story retold and relived by so many of the game's greats, across South America, Africa, Eastern Europe and, for Gascoigne, on the streets of Dunston. He may have become a superstar through circumstance, but that was never his intention nor his desire. He was a football supporter who bridged the gap into professional football but continued to blur the lines between these two worlds until they could not be distinguished from one another. Had Gascoigne not been a footballer, he would have been partying with his mates, the joker of a group of men who followed their club and maximised the fun in doing it. He still did most of that even as a footballer.

The stories about Gascoigne's time in Rome are numerous and legendary, and some must be apocryphal. After his partner Sheryl returned to England, Gascoigne was protected by two bodyguards, Gianni and Augusto. The pair ended up being his guardians and close friends, but were always involved in his scrapes.

One night they burst into Gascoigne's apartment after hearing him scream, only to find a pair of shoes left in front of the balcony door to give the impression that he had jumped off onto the floor below. Cue Gascoigne, hidden in the bathroom, in fits of giggles. It prompted a gun to be pointed at Gascoigne's head until a promise came that the incident would not be repeated. Gascoigne also remembers Gianni and Augusto having responsibility for guarding a bank vault in Rome city centre, and persuading them to let him enter the vault and sit on the piles of money on the promise of not interfering with the notes. Needless to say, Gascoigne was soon throwing wads of cash into the air.

He also caused quite a stir on Rome's social scene, with the most famous tale coming when Gascoigne was dining in one of the city's most exclusive restaurants. Struggling to make the waiter understand what he wanted to order, Gascoigne dived into the lobster tank, grabbed his victim and handed it to the waiter to take to the kitchen. To repeat, the line between reality and apocrypha may be blurred. Still, a good story is a good story.

On the pitch, crucial to his cult-hero status was Gascoigne's reputation as a player who excelled in moments. His consistency of performance – and availability – might have fluctuated wildly in Rome, but the Pescara goal and late Roma equaliser were not just among the best moments of Gascoigne's season. They were Lazio's highlights as well. For better and worse, he has always had a habit of making sure the spotlight focused brightest and longest on him.

Gascoigne appreciated his role within the ecosystem of Lazio and Italian football. His job was not simply to train hard or score goals – and sometimes he didn't even manage that – but to entertain. As the great Liverpool manager Bill Shankly said when asked how he would like to be remembered: 'That I've been working for people honestly all along the line, for people in Liverpool that go to Anfield. That I've been working for them to try and give them entertainment.'

Gascoigne's ability to succeed in the role of clown prince made him popular not just with Lazio supporters but across Serie A. Atalanta fans created a banner for when they played Lazio with a huge bottle of beer and the welcome: 'This one is for you, Gazza,' and that was a fairly consistent message. Even Roma supporters, their weight jibes aside, would concede that Gascoigne was a wonderful character to have at a club.

If Lazio's aim when buying Gascoigne was to buy a player who would make their supporters love the club a little bit more than they had before, then it was a roaring success. At every home game at the Stadio Olimpico since he departed, there has been a banner on the Curva Nord bearing Gascoigne's image.

If Gascoigne's popularity with Lazio's supporters was never in doubt, his relationship with some of his teammates was far less certain. Italian footballers hardly have a reputation for glumness, but the stereotype is that they pride themselves on professionalism and personal fitness. As Alex Ferguson is quoted as saying in Gabriele Marcotti's *The Italian Job*, Italian players have – or at least had – a greater respect than the English for their profession: 'They enter a system that has a certain discipline, and it has been that way in Italy for thirty to forty years. Clubs elsewhere copied the Italians.'

If there were times when Gascoigne was a professional by technicality rather than behaviour, was there not a chance that his antics might antagonise his teammates? Does a dressing room really need a clown when the business of winning is so serious?

Yet here again, the strength and warmth of Gascoigne's humanity won out. With the exception of Germans Thomas Doll and Karl-Heinz Riedle, who reportedly complained to the club that Gascoigne was being afforded special treatment, there is almost no insinuation that Gascoigne was anything other than a highly popular teammate.

Perhaps this is because the other players didn't actually tend to socialise much with Gascoigne, or because he was a perfect lightning rod for media intrusion in a country where cameras and microphones continually invade the personal space of famous footballers. But most likely it is because Gascoigne was – and is – a man it's impossible to dislike, a vulnerable soul but a kind and generous one too.

Still, there must have been times when Gascoigne's joker persona tested the patience of his teammates. One well-known tale concerns Roberto Di Matteo, who reached into his pocket after Gascoigne had asked to borrow some change and found his hand making contact with a live snake. Gascoigne had found it in the garden of his villa after the morning training session and realised it could be the perfect prop for an afternoon practical joke.

When appointed Chelsea manager in 2012 Di Matteo recalled the incident, and his disbelief still lingered: 'I think anybody would react! I didn't think he was that crazy to put a live snake into my pocket. I didn't go near it because I'm so afraid of snakes. He did a lot of things, a lot of stuff, my God, some crazy stuff.'

There was also an occasion when Gascoigne had not turned up for training. As the team bus pulled into the training ground, he was seen lying by the side of the road with a motorbike on top of him, covered in blood. It was not until several teammates had run to his side that Gascoigne burst out laughing, stood up and pointed to a large amount of tomato ketchup on his clothes. The Italian players must have wondered who on earth had arrived at their club.

'He was a man with the heart and the eyes of a child,' said Pierluigi Casiraghi, probably intending that as both compliment and insult. 'We were on the team bus once and he sat down behind Zoff. As soon as the bus went into a dark tunnel, he stripped off all of his clothes and just sat there, waiting for Zoff to turn around and see him naked.'

Yet most obvious in the anecdotes of his Lazio teammates is the unanimous surprise not at Gascoigne's japery, but his extreme generosity. It became a tradition for him to present the squad's younger members with presents. Alessandro Nesta recalls being given five pairs of shoes and a fishing kit, while Gascoigne gave Marco Di Vaio an expensive camera. Gascoigne was not a materialistic person, but he understood that others took pride in their possessions. His natural reaction was therefore to give things away to make others happy.

'No one could ever dislike Paul. He was so generous,' said Signori, still a friend of Gascoigne today. 'If you ever said, "Gazza, what a beautiful watch, where did you buy it?", he would take it off and give it to you.'

If Lazio supporters were quickly falling in love with their new English star, there was an Italian football revolution happening back home too. Exactly as at the Stadio Olimpico, Gascoigne was the poster child for the movement.

The 1990 World Cup did not just change the perception of the England team abroad and at home; it also altered the English public's preconceptions about Italian football. We had been told that it was a league of stupefyingly dull matches played by teams who focused too heavily on *caten-accio* – safety-first football.

The reputation was extreme but had a basis in reality. In 1986/87 Napoli won Serie A by scoring just forty-one times in thirty league games. They were the top scorers in the division. Only eighth-placed Avellino and Udinese, who finished bottom, conceded more than thirty-five league goals. Even Italia 90 itself contained fewer goals per game than any World Cup before or since, although the fault there hardly lies with Italian football.

And yet that tournament captivated the English public. The crowds were fervent and the pictures beamed back had a technicolour hue, persuading us that there was a rich footballing culture beyond our shores. Crucially, we wanted to continue our long-distance love affair.

The summer of 1992 ushered in a new era of English football. The breakaway of the Premier League, funded and fuelled by the advent of satellite broadcasting thanks to BSkyB, took top-flight English football away from our terrestrial screens. The days of live broadcasts on Sky Sports and BT Sport of thirty or more matches from as many as eight different countries every weekend, supplemented by innumerable matches from almost every continent of the world on betting streams, might as well have been light years away. Instead, we were forced to settle for live weekend broadcasts from Second Division grounds.

The new Premier League product took a while to get going. English clubs struggled in Europe following the lifting of the Heysel ban as they quickly realised that they were now playing catch-up with their continental peers, while the league itself hardly changed overnight. This was First Division football, gold-plated and rolled in glitter. And we were asked to pay for the privilege of watching it occasionally glint in the sunshine.

The timing was perfect. Neil Duncanson was a TV executive working for Chrysalis and was making a documentary about Gascoigne's recovery from serious injury. With England's star attraction closing in on his move to Italy and commenting to Duncanson that it was a shame English viewers would not see his performances live, Duncanson had his lightbulb moment. He initially asked the Italian Football Federation to show only Lazio's matches, but was told it was all or nothing.

'We thought, hang on: Sky are about to nick everything and we can get the rights for £700,000,' he told the *Guardian* in 2012. 'I spoke to Michael Grade, who loved the idea, and we did a deal. At the time Sky had posters all over Britain saying: "Watch the Premier League live and exclusive on Sky Sports." Grade then went and bought every poster site next to them and put up a different poster: "Watch the World's Premier League live and exclusive on Channel 4."'

Initial take-up on Sky subscriptions was slow, and so relatively few people anticipated watching televised top-flight football. Channel 4's new offering, *Football Italia*, afforded the English public a chance to watch the best players in the world for free, every week. In 1992/93 the top ten Serie A scorers were Signori, Roberto Baggio, Abel Balbo, Rubén Sosa, Gabriel Batistuta, Daniel Fonseca, Roberto Mancini, Maurizio Ganz, Jean-Pierre Papin, Florin Răducioiu and Marco van Basten. The Premier League's top ten included Brian Deane, Paul Wilkinson, David White, Micky Quinn, Chris Armstrong and Dean Holdsworth. It was a no-brainer for Chrysalis and for the viewer.

Three million people watched the first Serie A match screened on British television, a 3–3 draw between Sampdoria and Lazio for which Gascoigne was not yet match-fit. The following week, Milan beat Pescara 5–4. It was as if Italian football as one understood the need to refute its established reputation and was determined to put on a show. Channel 4 drew in four times as many viewers for Serie A as Sky did for the Premier League during that first season. Given the initial Anglo-centric nature of the idea, the most pleasant surprise was that the biggest audiences were not for matches involving English players.

If the live coverage could speak for itself, bar the odd maniacal montage and shouted message of '*Campionato! Di Calcio! Italiano!*', Channel 4 also produced a Saturday morning show they named *Gazzetta Football Italia*. It was a quasi-reality TV/magazine show that also showed highlights of the previous weekend's matches, and it was here that cult status was truly achieved.

Gascoigne was originally intended to present *Gazzetta*, but it quickly became clear that he was hardly the most reliable host. Instead, an arrangement was reached whereby he would be involved with various sketches and skits within the programme, generally designed to send him up but with Gascoigne a perfectly willing participant in the fun. He would be broadcast with his head inside a giant chocolate egg, walking around a zoo with a python around his neck or having salacious sexual predilections insinuated. Gascoigne giggled throughout, and the audience laughed with him. *Gazzetta* was a sensational hit.

Gascoigne being Gascoigne – or perhaps Gascoigne being Gazza – he roped plenty of Serie A's other stars into proceedings. David Platt appeared dressed as the Terminator, Gianluca Vialli wore a wig and Attilio Lombardo danced the lambada, just because. The popularity of the shows led to cameos from Ardal O'Hanlon, Bryan Adams and Elvis Costello.

The legacy of *Gazzetta* and *Football Italia* lives on. They inspired a culture of European football weekends and Championship Manager and helped create the audience – and shape the coverage – of televised foreign football today. As Sean Ingle wrote in the *Guardian*, '*Gazzetta* became as much a part of people's Saturday mornings as a stomach-settling full English.' It earned the highest ratings ever by a Saturday morning show for Channel 4.

'I don't think I've had such warmth given to any show I've ever made,' Duncanson says. 'I remember Ian Wright saying to me that every football player he knew watched *Gazzetta* on a Saturday and *Football Italia* on a Sunday. But I knew we had cracked it when I was walking around a park and someone scored and wheeled away shouting: "Golazzo!"'

It was also vital for Gascoigne. More than simply filling some of his time in Rome, his role in *Gazzetta* gave him a link back to England outside of the fleeting international appearances. When he told Duncanson that it was a shame the English public wouldn't get to see him play, he was thinking of himself as well as them. Being isolated from his people was his biggest fear about moving to Italy. Now they could watch him perform for Lazio fans on a Sunday afternoon, and for them on a Saturday morning. Gascoigne the entertainer, in more ways than one.

SOTTO I RIFLETTORI

*The media glare, the belch
heard round the world*

Gascoigne rarely dealt well with authority. A psychologist might suggest that this was the natural result of a combustible relationship with his mother, with whom Gascoigne remembers having blazing rows that often included physical violence. He also witnessed domestic violence between his siblings, and regularly received the slipper treatment when misbehaving.

Playing football was Gascoigne's release from the difficulties of his childhood, but the reality of professional sport is a world away from the idyll of kicking a ball around for pleasure. There are coaches telling you how to train, managers telling you how to play and directors telling you how to behave. Gascoigne often felt that certain characters in each of those roles stymied his natural joy for the game. Italian football had far more structure than the English game he had left behind.

Gascoigne was at his best when given compassion and love by his managers. If the argument is that special treatment should not be afforded to a professional footballer, such rigidity is unhelpful in practice. Teachers are supposed to treat all children equally, but the best soon learn that some require hand-holding while others are best left to their own devices. The same is true of football managers.

There is no doubt which manager got the best out of Gascoigne, and it was no coincidence that he was the manager who also had the closest personal connection with him and thus gained his trust. In *Glorious*, Gascoigne recalls how he made a dreadful mistake that led to the concession of a goal in England's last warm-up game before Italia 90:

> At the end of the match I was very low, and Bobby showed how brilliant he was. He recognised the state I was in and knew me enough then to realise I would let it eat away at me, so he put his arm around me and said, 'Don't worry about it, Paul. You'll be fine.' That was all I needed.

That is proof that Gascoigne did not need special treatment in the sense of hours of micro-management. He simply reacted well to managers who bothered to get to know him, understood the quirks of his personality and made timely gestures to allay any festering misgivings. Show Gascoigne that you were a caring person, and he was on your side.

Several years after Robson passed away, Gascoigne spoke on a charity DVD, *A Knight to Remember*, to give his memories of his former manager, mentor and friend. 'Before he passed away, I played in an England–Germany charity match,' Gascoigne said. 'Sir Bobby was there in his wheelchair and I went up to him to say, "Boss, it's Gazza." He was still a bit drugged up with the morphine. He had to leave early, but his son told me later that he asked, "How did Gazza do?" That was quite heartbreaking. God, he still remembers. So many times I think about him . . . those last words about me.' By now, tears were flowing down Gascoigne's cheeks.

Zoff, Gascoigne's first manager at Lazio, did not have the patience – or perhaps even the inclination – to deal with Gascoigne in exactly the same way as Robson. 'As a coach, you have eleven people to worry about, there is no time for anything else, and you can never be completely at ease,' he told the *Independent* in October 1992, a month after Gascoigne had joined. 'Ask anyone in Italy. Zoff is a serious man. I have no time to relax and be anything else.'

That was hardly to Zoff's chagrin; it was all he knew. Italian football was not used to indulging players, even those with supreme natural talent. The expectation was that every player would be committed to their own personal fitness and maximising their potential on the pitch. It is exactly how Zoff had established himself as one of the greatest goal-keepers of all time, having been rejected five times as a youngster.

It is untrue to say that Zoff did not like Gascoigne; quite the opposite. He initially wanted to make his midfielder the captain of his side, believing he would flourish given that responsibility, and later described Gascoigne as one of the best players he had ever worked with.

But rather than offering him a consoling arm around the shoulder, Zoff left Gascoigne to his own devices, explicitly telling him that he could drink as long as his performance level stayed high. There are doubts whether Zoff was the type of personality to whom you could go with an emotional issue and talk it through. That said, very few managers in the early 1990s were.

What is certainly true is that there were no doubts about Gascoigne's behaviour at first. Again speaking to the *Independent* in October 1992, Zoff described him as being a model professional, albeit leaving open the possibility of future hurdles to jump:

Now is not the time to worry about him being a playboy. He is working like a dedicated professional and is down to 79 kilos – his best weight. When he is playing as well as he used to, and becomes the best player in Italy, that's when the distractions will be there.

Gradually, Zoff's relationship with Gascoigne took on the character of a weary mother looking after a slightly mischievous child. 'I loved that boy,' he beamed in an interview with the *Daily Telegraph* in 2002. 'He was a genius, an artist. But he made me tear my hair out. The pity was we saw the beauty he was capable of only so rarely. He destroyed that beauty.'

Gascoigne's mistake was failing to understand the 'time and place' rule of his japes, or perhaps just not possessing the mental mechanisms to even recognise these as concepts. Zoff tells a story about bursting into laughter after Gascoigne entered the team dining room completely naked having been told to come to dinner straight away by his manager, and there is clearly warmth in his memories of those incidents.

'We'd all just finished eating, the team's gathered together and there are other hotel guests in the dining room,' Zoff explained. 'Suddenly, the door opens and Gazza, totally naked, walks through the room like it's the most natural thing in the world. He comes up to me and says: "Here I am, boss. Manzini told me to come straight away, just as I was." I couldn't think of anything to say to him, so I simply burst out laughing.'

Over time, however, it began to wear. The first issue came after Gascoigne's third game for his new club, the 5–3 defeat to Milan in which Lazio were outclassed by the reigning – and eventual – champions. Gascoigne, hurt by the comprehensive nature of the defeat, let rip at his teammates for not fighting hard enough and possessing insufficient quality to compete. '*Stai zitto. Tu non capisci uncazzo del calcio Italiano*,' was Zoff's angry response to Gascoigne. Shut up. You know fuck all about Italian football.

And then came the repeated practical jokes. One story that Gascoigne shares is that he was told by Zoff that then-FIFA general secretary Sepp Blatter would be visiting the club's training ground, and that every player must be on time. Gascoigne did indeed stick to Zoff's request, but wore a full Santa Claus outfit and marched up to Blatter to introduce himself as St Nicholas. Zoff's understandable anger and embarrassment led to extra training sessions for Santa.

The most significant falling out in Gascoigne's first season came when he was selected for a mid-season benefit match against Sevilla, a few days after recovering from flu. Gascoigne had not played in the league game two days previously, and was put out by the insinuation that he was being saved for the money-making exercise. He flew to EuroDisney in Paris with partner Sheryl and her two children instead.

When the club rang Gascoigne and told him that they would pay him a significant sum of money to appear in the game, he agreed to fly back to Rome and played. But Gascoigne then discovered that the club had lied to him about the appearance fee and would instead be fining him for his unauthorised holiday. Telling Zoff to 'Fuck off' and that he would leave the club did not go down well.

If Zoff at least understood the benefits of treating Gascoigne differently and made efforts to get on well with his English midfielder, club president Cragnotti's relationship with him was a little more difficult. This might have stemmed from the initial delays in the move, and Cragnotti's (quite reasonable) belief that Gascoigne owed him and Lazio consistent professionalism, given how understanding the club were over his injuries.

In Gascoigne's defence, he had hardly kept his antics a secret from Cragnotti. When general manager Manzini came to watch him in recovery training at Tottenham, a youth team player was sent to get Manzini a hot drink. Gascoigne's bright idea was to get his air rifle – as you do – and shoot the teapot from the tray that the player was carrying towards Manzini.

Gascoigne soon crossed the line in the eyes of president Cragnotti. His first faux pas came when driving through Rome near the Stadio Olimpico, with supporters surrounding his car. In his attempt to extricate himself from the crowds, Gascoigne ran over the leg of one supporter, leaving tyre marks and serious bruising. He gave the man his shirt as a means of tempering the situation, but the fan gave interviews to the press and Gascoigne received strong words from Cragnotti.

When Cragnotti visited the club's training ground one day with a host of club officials, Gascoigne approached him and uttered the words, '*Tua figlia, grande tette*' ('Your daughter has big tits'). While the club officials stifled giggles, Cragnotti was understandably less than amused. Having your daughter treated as a sexual object by your record signing in front of your colleagues isn't a great look for a business mogul and club owner.

Worse was to come. In January 1993 Lazio hosted Juventus at the Stadio Olimpico in a game for which Gascoigne was injured. Before the match began, Gascoigne was sitting with England teammate David Platt – who played for Juventus at the time and was also injured – in the seats reserved for players and club officials. Players were not permitted by the club to talk to the press before the game, but a journalist from *RAI Sport* attempted to source a quote from Gascoigne.

The obvious response, for anyone else at least, would have been to smile politely and ignore the question or offer a non-committal noise to indicate that no comment would be given. In his wisdom, Gascoigne let out a burp that was broadcast live to the country on primetime television, and replayed thousands of times over the subsequent days and weeks.

It was the dimmest thing Gascoigne could have done. It may have been a silly, thoughtless joke to him, but the Italian public were horrified. The incident was debated in the Italian parliament and the minister for tourism was asked to conduct an official enquiry. The insinuation – and you can see the point – was that Gascoigne was mocking Italian culture and the industry that was paying his wages.

Were an Italian to do the same, there would be an outcry. But for a foreign footballer to disrespect his new country of residence was a scandal. Even Zoff, predisposed to defend Gascoigne at that time, admitted that 'It was not a good way to behave.' What else could he say?

Cragnotti was apoplectic. Not only had Gascoigne let himself down on national television, he had also brought the name of his club into disrepute. He had been wearing his Lazio club blazer, sitting in Lazio's VIP seats in Lazio's stadium. Gascoigne was summoned to meet the president for lunch, where he had the riot act read to him about what it meant to be a Lazio player and the standards that would be expected of him.

Gascoigne was fined £9,000 by the club, and the memory of that belch would last for a long time in Cragnotti's mind. He had taken a chance on Gascoigne, sticking with him despite injury, paying an unprecedented transfer fee and allowing the player to negotiate a higher salary than Cragnotti had intended. This was evidence, he felt, of Gascoigne throwing that trust back in his face. Injuries could be forgiven, for they were no fault of Gascoigne's. But insolence was to be frowned upon, and forgiveness came less easy on that charge.

'He is uncontrollable at the moment,' Cragnotti would eventually say in April 1994. 'He must understand that we live in a professional world where everyone wants to win. I have invested a lot of money, and this is an investment that should be respected.'

It was a world away from Cragnotti's glowing assessment of a year earlier: 'Whoever wants our Gazza should give up the idea that he will become available. He will be staying in Rome forever.'

If Cragnotti's outrage caught Gascoigne by surprise, it was nothing in comparison with the media fervour. 'In the highly paid world of Italian football, certain behaviour is not tolerated,' an *Independent* column read. 'Gazza has damaged the image of English football and that of the English.'

The belch made front-page headlines for days in Italy, and pundits continued to analyse and denounce Gascoigne's behaviour. His sending-off against Genoa five weeks later, just as the storm was dying down, only gave them more ammunition.

Gascoigne had always harboured a deep mistrust of the written press, bar the odd individual exception. He believed them to be both parasitic and two-faced, hanging on to the coat-tails of his career in order to make money and offering faux-friendly words when they wanted an interview, only to crucify him at the drop of a hat and the lack of a back page. Furthermore, Gascoigne could not understand – or failed to remember – that everything he said would become a story. The press knew that if they hounded him for long enough that a story would fall into their laps.

You can see both sides of the equation. Gascoigne hated the media intrusion, and there is no doubt that it went far beyond the pale of what is acceptable. There would be photographers camped outside his villa in Rome, taking pictures of Gascoigne and topless shots of Sheryl. And yet the media knew that the English public wanted to read about Gascoigne. Gazzamania was best reflected in the fascination for newspaper copy about Gascoigne on and off the pitch.

If Gascoigne thought that the English media were intrusive, it was nothing compared to the saturation coverage of football in the Italian press. Rather than simply the back pages to fill, Italy had – and still has – three sport-specific daily papers, *La Gazzetta dello Sport*, *Corriere dello Sport* and *Tuttosport*; that's an awful lot of space for conjecture and sensationalism. This again raises the question of whether being a professional footballer in Italy, with its media circus, was the right move for Gascoigne.

Gascoigne's problem – although he can hardly be criticised for the move – was to refuse to play the media game. During Italia 90, when many England players were refusing to speak to the English press over their treatment of the squad and its manager, Italian papers submitted questions to Gascoigne in written form. Gascoigne returning them with one-word answers was viewed as a declaration of war.

The truth is that the Italian media was out to paint Gascoigne as an unfit English yob who did not merit the special status afforded to him by supporters and managers. Sadly, incidents such as the pre-Juventus belch only legitimised the extremity of their coverage.

There were other times when Gascoigne failed to make friends in the press. He met one reporter on a plane who had said some less than complimentary things about him a few months earlier. Gascoigne punched the man in the genitals with enough force that the reporter threatened to involve the police (although he never did).

Later on, Gascoigne describes being out shopping with Sheryl when a photographer became particularly intrusive when taking pictures of the pair. Having told the photographer that he would hit him if he was still there when he came out of the shop, when he found the man in exactly the same place, Gascoigne punched him in the face. This time the police were called and Gascoigne was forced to give a statement. Unsurprisingly, the story made headlines in the press.

Both of these incidents share a common characteristic: namely that Gascoigne had established a position of moral high ground only to cede it through his own misguided actions; see too the first punch in Newcastle to protect his sister. Gascoigne was never a cruel man – at least not when sober – and his physical attacks on members of the media were a means of protecting himself and those close to him. He could not understand why he was being followed wherever he went, and he begged for privacy.

Later Gascoigne would tell a UK court, having had his mobile phone hacked by titles within Mirror Group Newspapers, that the paranoia caused by media intrusion exacerbated his alcoholism and drove him to the edge of suicide. He eventually settled for significant damages.

'At the time I was going through a bad time because I knew I was getting hacked. I knew 110 per cent. No one believed it,' Gascoigne said. 'I was speaking to a therapist and it clicked again. He told me I'm paranoid, I'm going through a mental disorder.

'I said: "There's fuck-all wrong with me." I know I'm getting hacked. I know and he put the phone down on us. I never told a lie. I've got nothing to lie about. Nothing. I've waited fifteen years to be sat here. I'm disgusted really. Fifteen years. Can I say one final thing? I'd like to trade my mobile in for a coffin because those guys have ruined my life.'

While you can never condone violence, even when he was in Italy Gascoigne was a man being pushed to the edge by those who knew precisely what they were doing, and who would then cry foul when they provoked their intended reaction.

It became a vicious cycle for Gascoigne. He felt the press were out to get him and that they would publish half-truths and rumours sold to make him look bad. Cragnotti would be angered by the club's name being brought into disrepute, which in turn would filter down to manager Zoff. It would never change his standing among Lazio supporters, but there is no doubt Gascoigne's reputation did suffer with Lazio's decision-makers as his time in Italy passed by.

LA GIUSTA FORMA

Weight problems,
flashes of brilliance

The journey of the word 'amateur' in a sporting context is an interesting one. Traditionally it was used to describe the Corinthian spirit displayed in games played purely for pleasure. Over time, however, it has taken on a negative connotation, used as an insult to attack professionals for their mistakes. Bad defending, naive decision-making and missed chances – all these can be 'amateur'.

The etymology of amateur is 'lover of', referring to the personality of the participant rather than their proficiency. It describes perfectly Gascoigne's approach to football. He loved playing with the ball at his feet because of the way it made him feel. Or, perhaps more accurately, the way it stopped him from feeling.

Gascoigne was a natural footballer but never a natural athlete. He didn't see the point of arduous training sessions and individual fitness programmes, partly because he didn't believe they helped his game but also because he could not derive any joy from them. For Gascoigne, football was something to be enjoyed, not endured.

In that sense, it's hardly surprising that the culture of Italian football training came as a huge shock to him. This is the country of the Milan lab that extended the careers of

Milan players during the 2000s – Paolo Maldini (40), Filippo Inzaghi (38), Cafu (38), Serginho (37) and Giuseppe Favalli (38), to name just five. Founded by Jean-Pierre Meersseman, it combined kinesiology, chiropractice and more conventional medical procedures to astounding effect.

Italian football in general prides itself on the longevity of its players. Eight of the ten oldest players who have started for the Italian national team have done so since 2001. In England, only two have. That's partly because of Italy's Mediterranean diet and partly because of its disciplined approach to training. It's fair to say that neither came naturally to Gascoigne.

There is an argument that Gascoigne was simply *too* talented. Like the majestic snooker player Alex Higgins, and with obvious similarities to Diego Maradona, his natural ability was so great that practice and training were rendered virtually useless. Gascoigne's magic lay in the moments that seemed heaven-sent, not rehearsed. The dink over Hendry, the free-kick against Arsenal, the slalomed run against Pescara; these were moments that only Gascoigne on the pitch could manage. More importantly, such moments of splendour were not more or less likely to happen if Gascoigne worked hard in training – or at least that was certainly his belief.

'The training was like nothing I'd ever experienced,' Gascoigne said. 'They ran you into the ground before you even looked at a football. That was a huge culture shock for me.' In the Channel 4 documentary *Gazza's Italian Diaries* he revealed just how alien the training process was:

I thought training might have been a little easy, but it started off very hard. While I was running, people were slitting my finger and taking blood samples. I thought, 'God, what's this all about?' And then going to test centres, head wired up, heart wired up. It was incredible. I think I was more wired up than a satellite dish.

This story says less about Gascoigne and more about English football. Here was a player who had been a professional for seven years in England before moving to Italy, indicating just how deep in the dark ages our game had been before Arsène Wenger's arrival in 1996. It's hardly any wonder that no English club made it beyond the second round of the Champions League in the five years after the Heysel ban was lifted.

Yet Gascoigne cannot lay all the blame at the feet of others. He lacked the self-discipline to be left to his own devices, evidenced by his alarming tendency to put on weight. After his first season at Lazio, Zoff sent him off for the summer break but, aware of the danger, warned him against putting on weight. Having spent his holiday in Florida mostly eating and drinking things he shouldn't, Gascoigne returned to Italy and decided to go for a run a few days before pre-season training. Halfway through the run, he decided that piña coladas in a local bar were the answer. Manzini recalls:

Zoff told me to keep an eye on him during his holidays.
Paul went to Miami one summer and I used to have to

ring him up every day. He kept telling me everything was fine. The day he flew back, I turned up at the airport to meet him. I caught sight of this huge-looking guy and said to a copper standing next to me: 'Ha, he looks a bit like Gazza, doesn't he?' Then I realised it was him. He must have weighed 89 kilos.

There is another, more tragic tale. When Gascoigne got injured during his second season, Zoff told him to take a fortnight off and recuperate away from the chaos of Rome. To Zoff's surprise, Gascoigne pleaded not to be given a break, which the manager put down to over-sentimentality. The club then paid for an all-expenses paid trip to the Amalfi coast.

When Gascoigne returned from the fortnight's holiday considerably larger than when he had left, Zoff was furious. Gascoigne's response was melancholic: 'I told you not to send me on holiday, Signor Zoff.' There is a pathos to that line reminiscent of the tragic character of Lennie in *Of Mice and Men*. Gascoigne always meant well, but . . .

After Gascoigne's first summer break, Zoff ordered him to lose two stone in a month before he could be considered for team selection, something that Gascoigne only achieved thanks to an extreme dieting process that he used more than once to try to get match-fit for a new season.

'I like to go on a water diet, and that usually gets half a stone off,' he revealed in his autobiography. 'It's just water and lemon, plus a bit of maple syrup for energy. I throw a bit of cayenne pepper into the water to give it some sort of taste. I drink four litre bottles a day, all day long, for four days. On the fourth day, I'll have a chicken sandwich. I know it's a mad diet, but that's what I do.'

This astonishing starvation routine demonstrates both the extremes of Gascoigne's personality and the resolve he possessed to remain part of the Lazio first team. Given his salary and the commercial deals on top of that, spending the season on the sidelines would hardly have been disastrous, and there would still have been plenty of suitors from other clubs. But Gascoigne took Zoff's challenge as a personal crusade. His coach realised that by setting his prodigy missions against himself, he could inspire Gascoigne back to full fitness.

After all, the success of his second season depended on it. 'Next season, Gascoigne can be one of the Italian league's great players, but it's important he works on his conditioning,' said Milan coach Fabio Capello after a 2–2 draw in March 1993. 'He is strong and quick, gets away from players beautifully and has the talent to reach that mark. However, he must work hard every day on his fitness. At the moment he is OK, but he should do better.'

Like his debut season, 1993/94 was a confusing blend of injury-induced absences and spectacular moments, reinforcing his status as a cult hero for the *Irriducibili*. Having started both of the club's first two Serie A games, Gascoigne then went three months without completing ninety minutes and missed all four games of a UEFA Cup run that ended disappointingly at the hands of Portuguese side Boavista.

And yet just as the doubts were creeping in about Gascoigne's long-term fitness and status within Lazio's squad (Cragnotti had signed Croatian Alen Bokšić, and Serie A had a three-foreigner rule), he produced a virtuoso performance in a 3–1 home victory over Juventus in December 1993, scoring the clinching goal. After reported interest from Leeds United, this was Gascoigne's message that he was not ready to give up on Serie A. In the second half he dominated Antonio Conte in Juventus's midfield and overshadowed Roberto Baggio, the European Footballer of the Year elect, creating a series of chances for Bokšić.

'Paul played well, he gave everything he had and he managed to last the ninety minutes, but now it depends on him to improve his physical condition,' was Zoff's guarded praise, careful to remind Gascoigne of the need for consistency, but goalkeeper Luca Marchegiani was more effusive: 'I'm delighted for him, because he has suffered a lot through the unfair criticisms that have rained down on him.'

This display sparked the best month of Gascoigne's time in Italy. He was easily the best player on the pitch in the 1–1 draw at home to Sampdoria, and was given the captain's armband against Cremonese on 30 January after Roberto Cravero was substituted. It was the first time that Gascoigne had captained any team at senior level, and shows the trust that Zoff still had in his midfielder.

On 12 February Gascoigne scored direct from a free-kick on the far left edge of the penalty area past former teammate

Valerio Fiori. It was the final goal in a 4–0 home win (Signori scored a hat-trick) that pushed Lazio up into fifth place in Serie A, just two points behind Juventus in second.

Gascoigne's form in the latter half of 1993/94 was buoyed by the appointment of Terry Venables as England manager in January 1994, taking over from Graham Taylor after England's failure to reach the 1994 World Cup. Gascoigne respected Venables and had flourished under his stewardship at Tottenham before moving to Italy.

While his appointment as national team manager sparked controversy owing to his previous business dealings, Venables was Gascoigne's ideal choice. Taylor had been indecisive about how to get the best of Gascoigne or whether even to rely upon him at all, but Venables was in no doubt.

'Paul's game has definitely matured,' the new England manager said after watching Gascoigne in the Stadio Olimpico against Cagliari. 'He's passing the ball earlier when it is needed, running with it intelligently and mixing the two well. He seems to have learned a lot here. It's harder to mark him now. People used to know what he was going to attempt to do, and how to set about stopping him. Now when someone gets in tight on him, he's laying the ball off, and just when they think there's no point in marking him any more, he'll go at them. He's got a surprise up his sleeve.'

Gascoigne, who would later rank Venables as the best manager he played under, was delighted to have his old mentor watching him in such a capacity.

'Sunday was the first time I've ever been comfortable

when an England manager has been watching me,' he said. 'When Graham Taylor came, I always felt I had something to prove. Terry knows me, I've worked with him and I felt relaxed with him there and just wanted to put on a nice display.'

Gascoigne also agreed with Venables's post-Cagliari assessment of his form: 'I'm pleased with my fitness and the way I'm performing at the moment,' he said. 'I think everyone at Lazio is happy with me now.' The Italian experience had improved his appreciation of the game. 'I've learned how to mix it up. I'm running when I should run and passing when I should be passing. I've changed and improved.'

All was rosy. All was calm.

And yet, as so often during Gascoigne's career, fate was lurking around the next corner, waiting to spring a surprise and pull him back down. In March 1994, during a typically tumultuous Rome derby, Roma's Valter Bonacina cut Gascoigne down from behind with a cynical, premeditated revenge tackle. Injury absence would follow, and worse still was to come in April.

Still, Gascoigne's second season deserves to be sold as a success. It started with him overweight and unfit, and with Lazio's club doctor telling Zoff that he could not foresee Gascoigne matching the manager's fitness demands and that he would therefore struggle to break into the side. While Gascoigne only managed 1,300 league minutes, he continued to prove to his public that he was worth their patience. When Panini included a voting slip in each packet of stickers to determine who was the fans' favourite player in Serie A, it was Gascoigne, and not Baggio, Baresi, Maldini or van Basten, who came top.

IL PUNTO DEBOLE

Yo-yo diets, battles with addiction

Football would always be Gascoigne's escape. He loved the feeling of having a ball at his feet, playing in a team and beating his opponent, of feeling part of a wider collective. He flourished with the control he had, at truly excelling at something. In fact, you might say that the only time he truly had control was when crossing the white line.

Injury layoffs, holidays, end-of-season breaks; all were damaging to Gascoigne. Football – and the culture of being part of a team – was his crutch, what helped him keep it together. Remember his words upon returning from a two-week holiday grossly overweight: 'I told you not to send me on holiday, Signor Zoff.'

When he retired from playing, every day was suddenly empty for Gascoigne, and no amount of alcohol could fill that gap. When drink and football could not act as his crutch, there was nothing to keep his sanity in place. There were no answers.

And yet, in some ways, football was the worst thing for Gascoigne. Because he found mastering even the most technical aspects of the game so easy, it never required his hard work. That caused a subconscious complacency in his psyche that left him open to distractions.

Gascoigne was also at his best when acting on impulse, and was thus told by his managers to do precisely that. Many of his battles in later life were an indirect result of being hardwired to act impulsively. It worked for him on the pitch, but not off it.

There is another uncomfortable theory here that must be covered: Gascoigne's mental health issues made him a better footballer. This is certainly the view of former Tottenham and England teammate Gary Lineker, and few in the game knew him better.

'Part of his genius, part of his magnificence, is the fact that he was so vulnerable,' Lineker said. 'Without that vulnerable side, without that carefree side, without all the things that come with Gazza, I don't think Paul Gascoigne would have been the player that he was.' It is a tragic trade-off.

Gascoigne's off-field problems in Italy were exacerbated by him being surrounded by the wrong people, and the deterioration of his relationships with the right people. There is no one factor that lay at the root of his issues – that is not how mental health works – but the absence of Glenn Roeder from his Roman experience made more difference than most.

Roeder and Gascoigne were teammates at Newcastle United and formed a close bond, despite Roeder being ten years his senior. In a world of mates, Roeder was a true friend to Gascoigne, supporting him when he moved to London and sheltering him from media intrusion. He allowed Gascoigne to lean on him and prop himself up, both metaphorically and literally, acting as his minder as well as confidant.

Interestingly, Roeder later revealed that contrary to wide-spread belief, Gascoigne had never drunk heavily before leaving Newcastle for Tottenham. That part of his life only began in London, away from Roeder's gaze and without the company of those who would entertain him all afternoon. Gone was the innocence of life in the north-east.

'All this talk of Gazza being a heavy drinker when he was at Newcastle is rubbish,' Roeder said. 'There was a great atmosphere among the youth team when Gazza was part of it. They would train in the morning, then go down the snooker hall and play all afternoon. This was often followed by a Chinese on the way home. The only time they had a drink was on a Saturday night in one of the clubs, and then after three shandies they were all on their backs.'

When Lazio agreed a deal for Gascoigne, it was also agreed that Roeder would move with his wife and children as well and live near Gascoigne. Lazio would use him in an assistant coaching role to enable Roeder to gain experience in an industry that he considered his natural next step, which would have the added advantage of Gascoigne being more easily assimilated into life in Italy. Or, as Gascoigne put it, 'stop me from doing anything too daft'. Roeder had bought Italian phrasebooks and begun to pick up the language, making enquiries about schools in Rome for the children.

Unfortunately for Gascoigne, Roeder cancelled his plans to move to Rome after Gascoigne sustained his second serious injury in that Newcastle nightclub. He felt deeply let down after Gascoigne's promise to stay out of trouble and, despite Gascoigne's understandable protestations that the fight was not his fault, cut off contact with his friend.

If Roeder's absence left Gascoigne alone in Italy, the supporting cast failed to make up the difference. His partner Sheryl would move to Rome and into Gascoigne's villa, but the arrangement only lasted six months and never came close to domestic bliss.

Gascoigne readily accepts that he was a difficult house-mate, uncomfortable in his new situation, and that he took it out on Sheryl and the children. Without Roeder to absorb and assist with his professional worries, Gascoigne leant too firmly on Sheryl. They would often argue, and Gascoigne eventually paid for her to buy a house in Hertfordshire with the kids.

In Sheryl's place, Gascoigne had Jimmy 'Five Bellies' Gardner and Cyril Martin. Gascoigne had met Jimmy at school at the age of fourteen, and the pair quickly became a double act. It is not really true to say that Jimmy and Cyril got Gascoigne into scrapes, because he was a more than willing participant in all antics, but trouble would always find the trio. Each of the three was bad news for the other two.

The stories seem amusing on the surface, and have been retold down the years to a guffawing audience. The most famous is the mince pie tale, with Gascoigne adding faeces (his autobiography merely says 'shit', but later versions confirm that it was the produce of a cat) to some pies and placing them in the fridge. When the group got drunk together the following night, Gascoigne persuaded Jimmy and Cyril to microwave the pies and tuck in. Sadly, they did as he said.

There are more, with Gardner usually the butt of the joke. Gascoigne once placed a cat that used to hang around the garden of his villa (possibly his sidekick in the mince pie prank) on Jimmy's naked body and let it scratch his chest. On another occasion, Gascoigne drove into Jimmy with his car, knocking him over and causing injuries to his friend.

One of Gascoigne's favourite tricks was to book flights for Jimmy to come out to Rome from London but send him via destinations across the world as far-flung as Cambodia. If that doesn't portray a man heavy on time and money but light on entertainment, nothing will. Yet the tales of debauched antics barely covered up the truth: Gascoigne was a functioning alcoholic.

Gascoigne has been and always will be an addict. There are theories that people can move away from addiction, and these clearly have some merit, but such cures are typically prompted by a change of environment and/or receiving treatment. Some people simply have the traits of an addictive personality: impulsive and compulsive behaviour and a dis-position towards attention- and sensation-seeking, coupled with social alienation. Gascoigne ticks every box. This is not to belittle the power of addictive products, but some hosts are more willing than others.

If alcohol was Gascoigne's most obvious vice, it was not his only one. Look again at his water, lemon and maple syrup weight-loss routine; that is not simple dieting, but an addiction to getting fit. His son Regan described how he replaced alcohol with sweets and popcorn, while Gascoigne also took up golf after his playing career ended and immediately began playing morning and night. Here is a man so predisposed towards extreme behaviour that it becomes his only manner of behaving.

It is this predisposition that offers a rebuttal to the theory that being signed by Alex Ferguson at Manchester United (he was close to a move in 1988 but joined Tottenham) would have prevented Gascoigne's personal decline. The question has become English football's great 'What if?'.

But that entirely misunderstands the situation. Gascoigne's biggest enemies were free time and money. Even the omniscient gaze of Ferguson could not have prevented Gascoigne's demons from taking over. The Scot might have temporarily stymied their rise, but hardwired personality always wins out in the end.

Telling tales of drinking would seem misplaced and distasteful, and this is not intended as a wart-and-all exposé, but there are two lines in Gascoigne's own books that stick out and bear repeating.

The first comes from Italia 90, when Gascoigne was the youngest player in the squad at twenty-three. There was a ban on England players drinking alcohol at their training camp before the tournament, but Gascoigne found a way around the issue. He describes ordering a cappuccino and a large mug of Baileys, and proceeding to scrape the foam off the coffee onto the top of the Baileys to cover up what he was drinking. Then comes the haunting line: 'I took a few sips and began to feel better almost immediately.'

The second relates to Gascoigne's poor fitness at the start of the 1993/94 season at Lazio, and his attempt at a jog before returning to pre-season training. Upon catching sight of the bar, deciding to postpone the fitness regime and ordering a piña colada, Gascoigne makes an admission: 'The thing is I like sweet things – piña coladas, for example – and once I have one, I can't stop.'

What is rarely spoken about in relation to Gascoigne is that his alcoholism was not the cause of his issues, but a symptom of them. In his autobiography he discussed having suicidal thoughts as early as the age of seven, how his father's illness provoked twitching and anxiety tendencies in him, and how he received psychiatric help after suffering from depression from the age of thirteen.

Having finally come to terms with his alcoholism after years of denial, Gascoigne is painfully honest about the reasons for his drinking, an admission that takes extraordinary courage. Even in a brief number of words, Gascoigne explains perfectly the circumstances and mental struggles that lead to dependence. His dependence happened to be alcohol.

'I've got an illness, I realise that now,' he says. 'It's not alcoholism, not really – that's more a result than a cause. What I've been suffering from my whole life is a disease in my head. I'm still scared of dying, that's part of it.

'Was life good beforehand? No, it wasn't. Getting

depressed is no fun. Getting drunk all the time to escape feeling depressed, now that I did like. What I didn't like was afterwards. I didn't like waking up in the morning, not remembering what happened, feeling ashamed and filthy and guilty. So overall, was life good? No, it fucking wasn't.'

Football as a community must take much of the blame for Gascoigne's issues. In the early 1990s, there was still an ingrained culture of drinking within most First Division clubs, and alcohol played a prominent role in squad morale. Some could cope with that culture without slipping into alcohol dependence; others couldn't.

The most devastating paradox of Gascoigne's career is that it was his majestic natural talent that facilitated his descent into alcohol dependency. His skill afforded him a myriad of second chances with club and country, but it also allowed managers to turn a blind eye to his personal problems. Zoff played a part in that too. Not long after he joined Lazio, the Italian levelled with Gascoigne: 'Paul, if you play well for me, you can drink as much beer as you like.'

That was an understandable stance, but also an incredibly damaging one. It taught Gascoigne that the negative impact of his drinking could be offset by his impact on the pitch. Actually, that was the worst possible way to address it. It causes enough problems when the addict themself masks the problem. When those around them, especially in positions of authority, do the same, it only reinforces a message of acceptance.

Therein lies the crippling lot of the artist: people are more interested in the 'wow' than the 'why'. As long as the results are good, the method is not questioned, even if it is suspected to be damaging. By the time Gascoigne first entered rehab in 1998 (signed in by the then-Middlesbrough manager Bryan Robson after drinking thirty-two shots of Scotch), his alcoholism was already entrenched.

'It is easy to forget just what a talent he was before the wheels fell off,' read an article in one English tabloid that offered an assessment of Gascoigne's career and life in 2016 and once again completely missed the point. Long after Gascoigne's retirement, his addiction was still being undermined by separating it from his playing career. The 'wheels had already fallen off' long before the end of Gascoigne's career. We were just too busy watching him drop a shoulder, dribble past an opponent and play the pass to notice.

To this unpleasant mix, we must add Gascoigne's own naivety. As an example, in *Glorious* Gascoigne describes how his lack of knowledge about recovery rates from injuries would lead to him phoning his former England captain Bryan Robson for advice.

'In later years, whenever I'd get an injury I'd call him up,' Gascoigne wrote. '"What now?" he'd ask. "I've done my arm in. How long will that take?" "Fucking hell, Gazza, it'll take about four-and-a-half weeks." Next one. "I've broke me leg."' This only reiterates the principle of Gascoigne as a wonderful amateur rather than a professional.

The reason for a comparatively high rate of addiction

among footballers is the game's capacity for extremes – from being adored by millions on a Saturday to an evening spent alone, and from a morning spent training with your mates to just another empty afternoon. The errant mind soon wanders. Gascoigne's low concentration span, lack of professionalism and high income created a toxic combination.

So football masked Gascoigne's mental illness rather than cured it. Too many people tried to separate Gascoigne the addict from Gascoigne the footballer, cheering one while censuring the other. To do so is to separate the footballer from the human being, turning players into circus animals with the remit only to entertain us. Money and fame provide no comfort blanket against mental illness. In fact, both can easily exacerbate the issue. A comfort blanket to keep you safe becomes a soundproof door to keep you quiet.

Gascoigne possessed none of the tools to deal with his stardom in Rome and, in hindsight, was never likely to come through unscathed. He was a famous footballer without protection, constantly surrounded by people on and off the pitch who benefited from his existence while simultaneously damaging it. Being wealthy, vulnerable and badly advised is a damaging blend for someone who is also achingly eager to please. Gascoigne was the man with a thousand mates but no friends. His mates drank with him; friends would have done anything but.

His problems were compounded by football's lack of a support network in the early 1990s. Depression is not a modern illness, but the recognition of it is restricted to the modern day. To reveal your mental illness in the testosterone-charged world of a Division One or Serie A dressing room would have been a concession or admission of weakness, not strength.

Depression would have been treated with an air of suspicion, or at least so many of its sufferers believed, being seen as an easy excuse rather than a debilitating and potentially life-threatening illness. Thankfully, attitudes are changing, and mercifully not too late for Gascoigne to have been understood.

Lazio are also complicit in this. They needed a success story to welcome in a new era of success and wealth but were not prepared to deal with Gascoigne's emotional baggage. His ability was something to be championed, but his personal defects were swept under the rug. To address them would be to investigate, and investigation would have produced undesirable answers.

'Looking back, I don't think too many people had Gazza's best interests at heart,' Jane Nottage said, although Gascoigne may accuse her of being the pot calling the kettle black. However, while the publication of her book was viewed by Gascoigne as a dereliction of her personal duty, on this issue she is right.

'We let him down,' she said. 'Everyone did, from the president downwards. People could have stopped the downward spiral but they didn't. Lazio wanted to keep him playing and, if they had sent him for psychoanalysis, they could have lost him as a player for months.'

Gascoigne's lack of a support network must extend beyond football and reflect badly on society in general. Drill down into any one of Gascoigne's extra-curricular incidents in Rome or at home, and it was clear that we were witnessing a soul in turmoil. If we had looked behind the eyes after every drink-fuelled escapade, we would have seen a man crying out for help. If Gascoigne wasn't strong enough to cry for help, society ought to have been in a position to offer it without request. It chose not to because Gascoigne was 'one of the lads'. His debauched character was celebrated – and still is, amazingly – even when it was obviously incredibly unhealthy.

This is the culture that we have created, where it is acceptable to watch a man's descent into the abyss all in the name of entertainment and, because he is male, he has been indoctrinated not to make a fuss. If someone has pneumonia, we help them. Why is depression any different?

Typically, it was Gascoigne himself who offered a candid and authoritative view on the subject. Speaking on *Good Morning Britain* in 2017, he said:

There are a lot of people who have got everything, but inside they don't share enough. There needs to be more done – especially with the guys. It's a macho thing. They think, 'Nah, I'm not doing this because no one will like me.'

Finally, Gascoigne's case poses questions for both the Italian and English media. Constant intrusion and microscopic interest would push anyone to the edge of distraction, but for those who are already struggling and who lack a support network, it can actively degrade mental health. Was any thought given to that eventuality? Did anybody care?

Not only did the press intrude upon Gascoigne's privacy without any consideration being given to his well-being, they also monetised his mental illness. Even if the argument of public interest stands up to the former – and that is open to debate – the latter becomes an issue of decency and morality. The same newspapers wishing Gascoigne well in his recovery must accept their culpability for his decline.

In this context, questions must again be raised about whether Italian football and Rome were the right move for Gascoigne, and this time answered. Did this bubble, away from his friends and surrounded by tag-along mates, exacerbate his decline?

It is certainly fair to surmise that Gascoigne was badly advised to make the move, particularly given that he was still overcoming the effects of serious injury, by those who had his – and their own – commercial interests at heart rather than his well-being. The financial rewards were significant, but so too was the impact of leaving his closest support network in England.

The honest answer is that it is impossible to say for sure. But it is tempting to conclude that, as with the Alex Ferguson conundrum, the where and when of Gascoigne's career were incidental to his problems of addiction. If the intrusion by the Italian media did indeed push Gascoigne down, he may well have fallen there anyway.

The truth is that Gascoigne was happy in Rome, or at least as superficially happy as his personal demons would allow. He took joy in being adored by Lazio supporters and his teammates, and felt huge pride in being named captain by Zoff. Had he avoided the fateful setback that befell him in April 1994, his Italian story could well have had a far happier ending.

FUORI ROSA

Zeman and the end of the dream

There are clear similarities between the two serious injuries of Gascoigne's career. Both came when he had been wound up to the point of frenzy. In 1991 the hype of the FA Cup Final and Gascoigne's last game in England led to his downfall. In 1994 he was angry at the squad being called in for a training session on a usual day off and riled by criticisms from teammates about his performances in a five-a-side game.

There is also something tragically fitting about Gascoigne's FA Cup Final cruciate injury and his 1994 broken leg both coming as a result of his own tempestuous tackles. It is rare for one serious injury to occur when the aggressor and victim are the same person, but for two such injuries to occur to the same person is virtually unique. Taken together, they offered an unheeded warning regarding Gascoigne's predisposition towards self-combustion.

Gascoigne's decision to dive into a challenge on young defender Alessandro Nesta was born out of frustration during a training session. As soon as the tackle was made, Nesta describes hearing Gascoigne's ghoulish screams and immediately understood that a serious injury had occurred. Nesta would continue to – wrongly – blame himself for the incident, although Gascoigne was quick to try to persuade him otherwise.

Gascoigne broke both his fibula and tibia, and describes feeling his leg where the bone should be and finding only a soft gap. The injury was so serious, and Gascoigne's past so chequered, that the headlines in the English press sold it on the back-handed compliment that Gascoigne's career was not expected to be over. If that's the good news . . .

The media reaction, as so often with Gascoigne, also brought out the worst in the English and Italian press. Gascoigne quickly made the decision to fly back to London from Rome to have the necessary operation performed by John Browett, the surgeon who had treated him in 1991 and 1992. As he was carried on a stretcher onto the plane, scuffles broke out between photographers and airline crew, who tried to confiscate their cameras. Gascoigne was hidden under a blanket, like a murder suspect hurried into court.

Gascoigne would have a steel rod temporarily fitted into his leg to aid the healing process, but he was ruled out of action for six to eight months. By October, Lazio club doctor Claudio Bartolini and Browett had both given the all-clear for Gascoigne to begin physical activity, but both advised against him literally and metaphorically running before he could walk. The most prescient words came from Enrico Bendoni, Lazio's vice-president: 'The psychological factor in Paul's recovery is very important. We will try to put him in the best situation for a speedy recovery without him having to suffer any other traumas.'

Perhaps if all had stayed the same in the Lazio coaching set-up during Gascoigne's absence, he might have been able to regain his place despite the layoff. After all, Gascoigne had done exactly that upon his arrival in Rome, the upside to his persistent injuries being that he was used to the physical ordeal of recovery.

But in the summer of 1994 Zoff was moved upstairs and into a sporting director role by Cragnotti. The change was not sold as a demotion for Zoff, but it was pretty clear that Lazio's president was after a speedy improvement despite finishes of fifth and fourth in his first two seasons. Elimination in the second round of both the Coppa Italia and UEFA Cup had done little to make Zoff's case.

Zoff's replacement was Zdeněk Zeman, a Czech-Italian coach who was born in Prague but had moved to Sicily in his early teenage years. Taking over at Foggia for a second time at the age of forty-two in 1989, Zeman had taken them from Serie C1 to the top half of Serie A, developing players such as Giuseppe Signori and preferring a distinctly un-Italian brand of attacking football. Understandably, Cragnotti liked what he saw.

The arrival of Zeman created two problems for Gascoigne. The first was that the new coach preferred to use a 4–3–3 formation, in which the two wingers or wide forwards were given the greatest freedom of expression. Previously, Gascoigne had been afforded that luxury in an advanced central midfield role, but Zeman used three central midfielders. One of these would have responsibilities as a deep-lying playmaker, a position that suited Gascoigne's skills, but Zeman expected all three to possess the stamina required to play box-to-box roles, helping out in defence before pushing forward into attack.

Stamina had never been Gascoigne's forte, but the physical demands of the role were particularly unrealistic given his recovery from serious injury. He became locked in a vicious circle of being unable to carry out that role and therefore not being selected, and then being unable to increase his match sharpness due to a lack of action.

Zeman also famously demanded total commitment in training, conforming to the Eastern European stereotype (despite Prague being considered Central Europe). Gascoigne claims that Zeman's methods angered the whole squad and caused complaints from Signori about the workload, but it's hardly a stretch to assume that he found it harder to adjust to than most.

It is a mistake to suggest that Gascoigne did not enjoy training; quite the contrary. He delighted in training sessions as they gave him an opportunity for social interaction with his teammates and the chance to have a kickabout – what indeed could be better? In fact, Gascoigne always professed to prefer the training schedule in Italy, with sessions in both mornings and afternoons, to the single morning sessions that were customary in England at the time.

The key to success with Gascoigne and training was to keep him entertained, again alluding to the school teacher/pupil analogy. You had to absorb him, and that was usually best done by putting a football at his feet as soon as possible.

Zoff hardly indulged Gascoigne in training. The Italian demanded hard work and would grow weary of any antics. But he also understood the benefit of skills training, shooting and small-sided games, in all of which Gascoigne flourished. Zeman was different, prioritising fitness to such an extent that Gascoigne felt alienated from the rest of the group. While he enjoyed training under Zoff, the same could not be said of his new Czech coach.

Zeman and Gascoigne got off on the wrong foot when the manager told him that he was overweight and must lose two stone before being considered for selection. As ever, Gascoigne threw himself into the mission. He explains how he cycled thirty-five miles a day and ran for a further eight for over two months in order to get his weight down, and eventually achieved the goal.

Yet that period was not without its issues. Gascoigne and Zeman notably clashed when the manager ordered him to do extra running after one long bike ride, and Gascoigne responded by taking four bikes and throwing them down the stairs at the club's training ground. It caused significant damage to the bikes and left Gascoigne with a bill from the club to replace them.

More significant was Gascoigne's claim that Lazio leaked the details of his lack of fitness to the Italian media. He believed it was in a bid from Zeman and Cragnotti to destabilise him, which if true was a low blow, particularly given that Lazio were well aware of the media agenda against

Gascoigne. At that point, Italy's press were more than happy to feast upon stories of Gascoigne's unprofessionalism. Very few gave him any hope of achieving his target weight.

An olive branch was offered by Zeman in early April. 'He's not yet ready to play for ninety minutes, but he's recovered and in good form,' he said of Gascoigne. 'He's a player of great technique, who can improve Lazio's play.'

But by the time Gascoigne had got back to full fitness, Zeman had moved him to the fringes of his first-team squad. In total in 1994/95 the midfielder would start only two league games and be introduced as a substitute in two others. His appearance from the bench with fifteen minutes remaining in the Rome derby in April 1995 was cheered vociferously by the Lazio supporters within the stadium, but they knew that the writing was on the wall. Gascoigne played just 223 league minutes in total; only three members of the first-team squad managed fewer.

Perhaps Zeman saw Gascoigne as a necessary casualty of his reign. As a new manager in his first major managerial role, the Czech needed to make a statement to his squad that he expected total commitment and discipline. Moving Gascoigne away from the first-team picture was an obvious move given his fitness problems, but it also drew a line in the sand. His English midfielder was not worth straying from his trusted 4–3–3 for.

Gascoigne would have had a stronger case for inclusion had Lazio been struggling in Serie A, but Zeman's arrival sparked a superb run of form that took the club to their highest league finish for over thirty years. Zeman's Lazio would never really challenge Juventus for the Scudetto, but they lost only one of their first ten league games and won their last five. That secured a UEFA Cup place for the following season.

Lazio also made significant progress in Europe, reaching the quarter-final of a continental competition for the first time since the lesser-known Coppa delle Alpi (Cup of the Alps) in 1971. They beat Dinamo Minsk, Trelleborg and Trabzonspor before being eliminated by a stoppage-time winner from Borussia Dortmund's Karl-Heinz Riedle, a former Lazio player, in the second leg in Germany.

Gascoigne's case was not helped by the 'three-foreigner rule' imposed upon European competition by UEFA and on Serie A by the Federazione Italiana Giuoco Calcio (Italian Football Association), and not abolished until December 1995. With Aron Winter in central midfield, new signing José Chamot in defence and Alen Bokšić up front, competition for non-domestic places was fierce. Chamot, who followed Zeman from Foggia to Lazio, and Winter both started twenty-eight league games, while Bokšić started twenty-two.

By the end of April, Zeman was dropping unsubtle hints to the waiting press. After a 0–0 draw against Cagliari, during which Gascoigne was introduced as a substitute with thirty minutes remaining but wholly failed to impress, Zeman said that he was 'pretty sure' that Gascoigne would be leaving the club to return to British football.

The manager did not sound angry, but weary: 'He can do no more for this club. He can't be our saviour, although I still consider him a great player.' The Cagliari draw would be Gascoigne's last appearance in Italian football.

Zeman's admission unsurprisingly sent the Italian newspapers into a fever. *Corriere dello Sport* was particularly scathing, writing that Gascoigne had been a disappointment, was finished at the highest level and would be having meetings with president Cragnotti over his immediate future.

It was not Cragnotti whom Gascoigne sought to clarify the rumours of his exit, but his old manager (and now sporting director) Zoff. Zoff confirmed that Lazio were indeed looking for a buyer, and presented Gascoigne with three potential options. What then followed was a moment of pure Gascoigne.

Chelsea, Aston Villa and Rangers were the three clubs interested in signing him, and are listed in the order of his initial preference. Having met Glenn Hoddle, Chelsea's manager, and Villa chairman Doug Ellis, and felt no significant urge to join either club, Zoff expressed his surprise that Gascoigne was not intrigued by Rangers' offer. It was not until he told his former coach that he had no interest in speaking to Queens Park Rangers that Zoff corrected him and explained that it was the Glasgow club that wanted him. Suddenly Walter Smith (manager) and David Murray (chairman) were in pole position. Gascoigne went on holiday and allowed agent Mel Stein to broker the deal. His exit from Italian football was being accelerated.

During his last week in Rome, Gascoigne fully entered dress-down-Friday mode. He drove to training on his Harley-Davidson motorbike and wore flip-flops and smoked a cigar as he entered the training complex. As he himself admits, 'There seemed little point in making an effort, so I just mucked around all week.'

His final day at training was bizarre, Gascoigne arriving already the worse for wear and mocking Zeman by lowering himself onto one knee and asking for 'the great one' for some words of advice. Gascoigne then fell to the ground, refused to move and was eventually carried to his car by Bokšić.

Bokšić would win the Scudetto and two Coppa Italias with Lazio, while Gascoigne won nothing. Here was the Croatian striker, in many ways Gascoigne's replacement as another exciting foreign addition, literally leading him away from the club. The symbolism should not be ignored.

L'EREDITÀ

The legacy

As Gascoigne appears outside the entrance to the tunnel, a gaggle of photographers gather around him, desperate to get a picture for one of the following morning's papers. Those at the back of the pack lift their cameras into the air in the style of a celebrity-hunting paparazzo, while others run further on, anticipating Gascoigne's next move and hoping to get a close-up shot. A few climb up onto the low wall of the stand, searching for higher ground and an angle. The interest in Gascoigne, Gazzamania, has never waned.

It is November 2012 and Gascoigne is back in Italy, back in Rome and back at the Stadio Olimpico. He is a guest of Lazio for their Europa League group stage game against Gascoigne's former club Tottenham. He had hoped to be present at the game at White Hart Lane two months earlier for similar treatment, but was forced to postpone. Gascoigne's well-being comes first, and he has endured unspeakably difficult times.

The timing could not be better. Six days after Gascoigne's homecoming in Rome will mark twenty years since his first goal for the club, that wonderful header to give Lazio a point in the Rome derby. Twenty years on, the *Irriducibili* still remember how that header momentarily put them on top of the world.

Gascoigne is given a hero's welcome, beyond all expectation. A collection of ball boys carry a 'Welcome home Gazza' banner across the running track in front of the Curva Nord, but there are many more held up in the stands. One has him wearing a Lazio shirt and smile with the Union Jack as a backdrop. Another displays a heartfelt message in English, held by at least fifty supporters as one: 'Lionhearted, headstrong, pure talent, real man. Still our hero.'

As Gascoigne finally makes it round the running track to the Curva Nord, he is still surrounded by photographers. It gives him the air of an Olympic 100m champion completing his lap of honour.

What is noticeable about the crowd of supporters who salute Gascoigne is just how young many of them are. Some cannot be more than twenty-two or twenty-three, which means they cannot have remembered anything about their English midfielder. But Gascoigne is a player and a person about whom stories are passed on. Those who never saw him play can still feel the connection.

Eventually Gascoigne stops and waves to those who are chanting his name repeatedly, the same words and tunes that were used twenty years earlier: 'Paul Gascoigne, la-la-la-la-la'. He is adorned with a light blue and white scarf, but most noticeable is the beaming grin across his face. This is not merely a former player going through the motions, but a man using an outpouring of love as a means of regeneration.

Those adoring supporters know that too. They are acutely aware that their former hero is suffering with the pain of mental illness and the disease of addiction, and is desperately fighting against both. They know that showing their respect and adoration for him really will make a difference. This is about football, of course, but it's about friendship too.

Even with a good helping of optimism, it would be inaccurate to say that Gascoigne conquered Italian football. In his *Calcio*, John Foot offers a sobering assessment of Gascoigne's impact on Serie A as a whole.

Foot recalls that in 2003 a video was released for the Italian football market with the title *Bidoni*. In Italian vernacular, *'bidoni'* refers to a rubbish (the Italian for a rubbish bin is *'bidone'*) player who was bought at a high cost and failed to perform. On the front cover of the *Bidoni* video stands Gascoigne, hands on hips.

Foot himself would describe Gascoigne's time as an 'unmitigated disaster', and there were equally severe words from Italian journalist Gianni Mura when Gascoigne left for Rangers in 1995: 'Perhaps Paul Gascoigne has finally gone back home. He has been one of the worst buys since the war. We anxiously wait the usual epilogue where he will criticise everyone and everything.'

But Foot also explains why that withering assessment was probably rooted in hardwired bias. To Italian football, Gascoigne was the boorish Brit who caused controversy far beyond his worth, and whose lack of professionalism played a part in the injuries that restricted his availability. He arrived at a time when Italians were predisposed to mistrust laddish English behaviour – particularly after the Heysel disaster.

Gascoigne provided them with enough material to entrench those views. The antics of Jimmy 'Five Bellies' Gardner, the belch and the disrespect shown to authority figures helped to shape the one-eyed assessment that Gascoigne came to Italy, won no trophies, played forty-three league games in three seasons and then slunk off back to Britain.

It's certainly true that Gascoigne's reputation improves with hindsight; time softens the edges. Because he was a player who produced spectacular moments that linger long in the mind – the equaliser against Roma, the goal against Pescara, the free-kick against Cagliari and the gallops over the advertising hoardings every time he scored – the less savoury incidents pale into insignificance. That is true not just of Gascoigne's time in Italy, but over his whole career. Captivation is sexier than consistency.

Yet Gascoigne was clearly influential in Italy, whether the country's media chooses to accept it or not. He helped to change the stereotype of England as a country of blood-and-thunder footballers. And such was the strength of his personality and role in their formation, it is very probable that *Football Italia* and *Gazzetta Football Italia* would not have happened without his move in 1992. Serie A would therefore not have had the cultural impact on British audiences that caused the boom in popularity of the league as a whole. That in turn removed some of the insularity of English football and helped to develop the Premier League too.

Yet for Gascoigne's true legacy, we must look not to Italian football as a whole but to Lazio as a club. The reception he received in 2012, twenty years after his arrival, is typically reserved for those who have played hundreds of matches or led their clubs to multiple trophies. For thousands of supporters to hold Gascoigne in such fond regard after just forty-three league matches is astounding.

That is partly about what Gascoigne represents. He might have barely been part of Zeman's team that finished second in Serie A, and have departed long before Sven-Göran Eriksson led Lazio to the Scudetto, two Coppa Italias and the Cup Winners' Cup, but Gascoigne marked the beginning of Lazio's golden era. He may not have performed at the level of Pavel Nedvěd, Christian Vieri or Marcelo Salas, but he was their forefather. In 1992 a club down on its luck really did sign the best young player in the world and the most talented English player of his generation.

Manzini, general manager at Lazio in Gascoigne's time and still in the same role today, is in the perfect position to reinforce that viewpoint. 'Paul Gascoigne is a mythical figure for Lazio fans and very popular in Italy,' he said. 'He was the first of a line of flair players who would take the club to success. There's always a corner of Tottenham in our hearts.'

But there is something far deeper to this than merely Gascoigne's place in the line of Lazio's flair players. Reputations are the forebears of legacies, and both are defined less by what you did and more by who you were.

It would be a stretch to say that Gascoigne immersed himself in Italian culture, but he did immerse himself in the fan culture of Italian football. Or, to be more accurate, Gascoigne and Italian football fan culture were made for each other.

Gascoigne is one of the kindest people you could ever meet, always happy to spend a minute or three with a supporter, sign autographs for waiting children and extraordinarily generous with his possessions and time. It was this extreme kindness that made Gascoigne so vulnerable. He saw the best in everyone and assumed that he would be treated as he treated others. Sadly, that was not always the case.

But Lazio supporters loved it. They adored the way Gascoigne celebrated each goal as if he had been born in Gianicolo rather than Gateshead, but also respected his propensity for mischief. There is no better way to establish yourself as a cult hero than by surrounding yourself with the people who pay to watch you perform. This is a man for whom airs and graces were an impossibility. Gascoigne did not need to ingratiate himself with supporters at any of his clubs, because he already was one of them.

Lazio fans also appreciated Gascoigne's commitment to recovery from serious injury to make his move a reality, and further dedication following his broken leg in 1994. For all the valid media concerns about Gascoigne's poor fitness due to his lifestyle, nobody could doubt his efforts to reintegrate himself in Zoff's and Zeman's plans.

Even those who eventually grew weary of Gascoigne's

problems, like Zoff, held an affection for him. 'Gascoigne made me tear my hair out at times,' he would later say. 'But I have a great affection for him precisely because he was an artist, and a genuinely nice lad.'

But the final words on Gascoigne's legacy are best left to two people, one who knew him well and one who would later learn of his impact. Claudio Lotito bought Lazio from Cragnotti in 2004, with the club facing bankruptcy following the downfall of Cragnotti's food empire. He was the man who walked Gascoigne round the Stadio Olimpico running track in 2012 and had Gascoigne plant kisses on his cheek for numerous photo opportunities.

'Paul represents an important part of the history of our club and it was an obligation on our part to invite him to the stadium,' Lotito said that evening. 'The affection of Lazio people for him has never ceased. He is one of the all-time favourites and still in the hearts of many fans because of his determination, character and the great games he played.'

And then there is Beppe Signori, Gascoigne's teammate and friend, and widely regarded as one of the best players in Lazio's history. The pair formed a bond on the pitch, but he was also Gascoigne's closest confidant off the pitch during his time in Italy.

'I don't believe that anyone who knew him well could have ever wished ill upon Paul,' Signori said. 'He demonstrated an incredible generosity with all his teammates and, when he was in the right physical condition he also showed he was a player who commanded the fee paid for him.'

The caveat in that assessment is important. When Gascoigne was fully fit, he was all that Lazio could have wished for. At his best, his performance level was beyond his teammates, as it would be throughout his career. But Lazio's supporters witnessed Gascoigne's best far too infrequently for his and their liking. This was a three-year exhibition of what might have been.

And what of Gascoigne himself? If Italy witnessed the best of him, allowing him to continue his Italia 90 dream and establish himself as a cult hero in a country that he held close to his heart, it also exacerbated his problems of isolation, alcohol dependence and media intrusion, while causing his division from those within his support network who had his best interests at heart. In particular, Roeder not joining him in Rome merits significant regret.

Still, this story deserves to be viewed through optimistic eyes. It cannot always be said of Gascoigne's life, but for a long while in Italy he was truly happy. How could he not be, when the outpouring of love from Lazio's supporters was so fervent and so genuine? Above all else – managers, presidents and teammates – it was the opinion of his public to which Gascoigne attributed the most importance. There are few players in the club's history whom Lazio fans have cared about more deeply.

Look again at that banner carried by the ball boys in 2012: 'Welcome home Gazza'. Gascoigne is the type of player and person who has five or six different 'homes': Newcastle, Tottenham, Lazio, Glasgow Rangers, Middlesbrough, at least. Supporters of each club would welcome him back as one of their own, for who he was as much as how he played. Gascoigne's personality is too infectious and his heart too kind for it to be any other way.

Gascoigne may have only lived in Italy for three difficult years, and been a part of first-team life for just two of those, but the length of his stay is beside the point. Wherever Gascoigne lays his boots feels like his natural home, to him and to those who adore him. If in twenty more years Gascoigne can be paraded around the Stadio Olimpico once more, the reception will still be as warm and heartfelt. You can be sure that he will wear the same scarf, wave the same wave and smile the same smile.

BIBLIOGRAPHY

Anon., 'Gascoigne poised to play on Sunday', *Independent* website, 4 April 1995.

Barlow, M., 'It was ice cream for breakfast and beer for lunch ... but as a player? Gazza was beautiful!', *MailOnline*, 19 September 2012.

Clarke, J., 'Italia 90: How the 1990 World Cup changed England', BBC website, 4 July 2015.

Cutmore, C., 'The glory days of Gazzetta Football Italia', *MailOnline*, 25 March 2018.

Davies, P., *All Played Out: Full Story of Italia '90* (Portsmouth, NH: Heinemann, 1990).

Duffy, S., 'Gazza – the talent, the tears and the road to perdition,' *Zani*, 11 May 2015.

Foot, J., *Calcio: A History of Italian Football* (New York: Harper Perennial, 2007).

FourFourTwo, 'Gazza, the untold stories: the need-to-know tales that launched a legend', FourFourTwo website, 17 April 2018.

—'Peter Beardsley: Perfect XI', FourFourTwo website, 28 July 2009.

Gascoigne, P., *Gazza: My Story* (London: Headline, 2005).

Gascoigne, P., *Glorious: My World, Football and Me* (London: Simon & Schuster, 2011).

Gascoigne, P. and McKeown, J., *Being Gazza: Tackling My Demons: My Journey to Hell and Back* (London: Headline, 2006).

Halliday, J., 'Paul Gascoigne says Mirror phone hacking drove him to severe paranoia', *Guardian* website, 11 March 2015.

Haylett, T., 'Gascoigne confounds the critics', *Independent* website, 16 March 1993.

Hayward, P., 'Gazza's downfall – Tottenham Hotspur, 1991', *Guardian* website, 18 May 2009.

Hodges-Ramon, L., 'The Roman tragicomedy of Paul Gascoigne at Lazio', *These Football Times*, 23 March 2018.

Hodgson, D., 'Gascoigne "fined" by shocked Lazio', *Independent* website, 27 January 1993.

Hytner, D., 'Paul Gascoigne heads for emotional reunion with Lazio fans', *Guardian* website, 22 November 2012.

Ingle, S., 'The days when Gazza was the ringleader in Channel 4's Italian job', *Guardian* website, 17 November 2012.

Jones, K., 'Tottenham in turmoil: Venables' bitterness at sour end to Sugar alliance', *Independent* website, 14 May 1999.

Kuper, S., *Football Against the Enemy* (London: Orion, 2003).

Lawrence, A., 'Why Italia 90 was not beautiful to everyone, but will always be special', *Guardian* website, 15 June 2015.

Lovejoy, J., 'Mature Gascoigne is key to Venables' master plan', *Independent* website, 15 February 1994.

—'Zoff's serious faith in Gascoigne and glory', *Independent* website, 23 October 1992.

Main, D., 'Sergio Cragnotti: The rise and fall of Lazio's Roman emperor', *The Gentleman Ultra*, 3 February 2017.

Marcotti, G. and Vialli, G., *The Italian Job* (New York: Bantam Books, 2007).

McKeever, S., 'Lazio: The Sergio Cragnotti era', *Outside of the Boot*, 6 August 2017.

Moxley, N., 'Paul Gascoigne was a must-see maverick and the game needs more characters like him', *Mirror Football*, 15 June 2015.

Moynihan, L., 'Paul Gascoigne: "I wanted to entertain the people"', *Shortlist*, date unknown.

Newman, P., 'Football: Gascoigne "out for eight months"' *Independent* website, 8 April 1994.

Nicholson, J., 'A Football365 love letter to ... Gazzetta Football Italia', *Football365*, 9 July 2017.

Nottage, J., *Paul Gascoigne: The Inside Story* (London: Collins-Willow, 1993).

Reid, S., 'The Zdeněk Zeman method: A look at the tactical approach of the legendary coach', *Outside of the Boot*, 27 November 2014.

Rich, T., 'The crying Caesar: Paul Gascoigne's Roman days', *Independent* website, 22 November 2012.

Riley, C., 'Lazio hint at Gascoigne's return', *Independent* website, 1 May 1995.

Scholar, I. and Bose, M., *Behind Closed Doors: Dreams and Nightmares at Spurs* (London: André Deutsch, 1992).

Sharma, R., 'A hero's welcome: Gazza's back at Lazio to watch Spurs ... and they STILL love him (despite his boozing, belching and that dodgy knee)', *MailOnline*, 22 November 2012.

Stewart, A., 'Gascoigne: Film review', *The Set Pieces*, date unknown.

Taylor, D., 'Gazza's Lazio debut – 20 years today', *Football Italia*, 27 September 2012.

Various, 'Gazza's moment of madness – 20 years on', BBC website, 4 May 2011.

Wheeler, C., 'Gazza's day of madness: It's 20 years on since the moment that defined a superstar's crazy career', *MailOnline*, 12 May 2011.

White, J., 'Paul Gascoigne was troubled even at his peak', *Daily Telegraph* website, 22 February 2008.

Winter, H., 'A glittering career tainted by turmoil', *Independent* website, 7 April 1994.